50 Walks in

YORKSHIRE
DALES

First published 2002
Researched and written by David Winpenny, Sheila Bowker and
John Morrison
Introduction by Chris Bagshaw

Produced by AA Publishing
© Automobile Association Developments Limited 2002
Illustrations © Automobile Association Developments Limited 2002
Reprinted 2004, Apr 2006
Reprinted 2007

Published by AA Publishing (a trading name of Automobile
Association Developments Limited, whose registered office is Fanum
House, Basing View, Basingstoke, Hampshire RG21 4EA.;
registered number 1878835)

Enabled by | Ordnance Survey This product includes mapping data licensed
from Ordnance Survey® with the permission of
the Controller of Her Majesty's Stationery Office.
© Crown copyright 2007. All rights reserved. Licence number
100021153

ISBN-10: 0-7495-3513-X
ISBN-13: 978-0-7495-3513-1

A CIP catalogue record for this book is available
from the British Library.

The contents of this book are believed correct at the time of printing.
Nevertheless, the publishers cannot be held responsible for any errors
or omissions or for changes in the details given in this book or for
the consequences of any reliance on the information it provides. This
does not affect your statutory rights. We have tried to ensure
accuracy in this book, but things do change and we would be grateful
if readers would advise us of any inaccuracies they may encounter.

We have taken all reasonable steps to ensure that these walks are
safe and achievable by walkers with a realistic level of fitness.
However, all outdoor activities involve a degree of risk and the
publishers accept no responsibility for any injuries caused to
readers whilst following these walks. For more advice on walking
safely see page 8. The mileage range shown on the front cover is
for guidance only – some walks may exceed or be less than these
distances.

Visit the AA Publishing website at www.theAA.com/travel

Paste-up and editorial by Outcrop Publishing Services Ltd, Cumbria
for AA Publishing

A03349

Colour reproduction by LC Repro
Printed in Italy by G. Canale & C. SpA, Torino, Italy

Legend

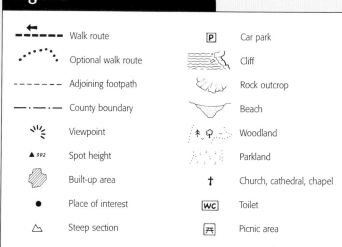

◄━━━━	Walk route	P	Car park
••••••	Optional walk route	∼∼∼	Cliff
------	Adjoining footpath		Rock outcrop
—·—·—	County boundary		Beach
☼	Viewpoint		Woodland
▲ 392	Spot height		Parkland
	Built-up area	†	Church, cathedral, chapel
●	Place of interest	WC	Toilet
△	Steep section	☴	Picnic area

Yorkshire Dales locator map

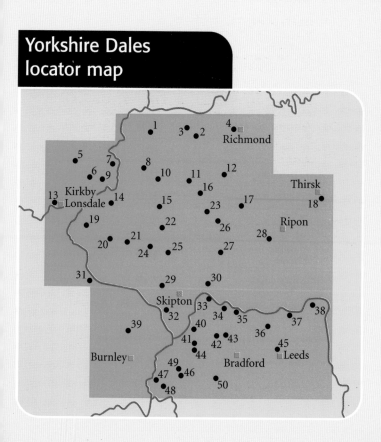

Contents

Contents

Rating: Each walk is rated for its relative difficulty compared to the other walks in this book. Walks marked 🚶🚶🚶 are likely to be shorter and easier with little total ascent. The hardest walks are marked 🚶🚶🚶 .

Walking in Safety: For advice and safety tips ➤ 8.

Introducing Yorkshire Dales

The Yorkshire Dales are a series of beautiful valleys spreading out from the high Pennine watershed to the north of the industrial heartlands of West Yorkshire. For the most part they are protected by the Yorkshire Dales National Park, which covers an area of some 684 square miles (1773sq km) across the upland centre of northern England. Dominated by an underlying geology of gritstone and limestone, the Dales attract thousands of visitors every year, many of whom come simply for the joy of walking among the quiet meadows or on the bracing moors and fells.

Swaledale

In the north, Swaledale is the most peaceful and least developed of these great valleys. It was once a centre for lead mining and hand knitting, but now tourists bring most of its income, attracted by the simple remote villages such as Reeth, Keld and Muker, and the breathtaking contrasts of light and dark, between the meadows and the brooding hills. Richmond and its great castle stand guard over the entrance to the dale, where the River Swale spills out into the lowlands of the Plain of York. In the tributary valley of Arkengarthdale, the landscape is littered with the scars of lead mining, but the abandoned workings have gently tumbled back in to the landscape and now add a fascinating historical dimension to walks in this remote area.

Wensleydale

Next comes Wensleydale, famous for its crumbly cheese and its ceaseless array of waterfalls, of which Aysgarth and Hardraw are the highlights. Even in the upper dale the scenery is less bleak than its northern neighbour, with larger villages like Bainbridge and Hawes serving as pretty urban honeypots. Over the watershed from here tumbles Dentdale, down to the cobbled village of Dent and the market town of Sedbergh. The map will tell you this is Cumbria, but the scenery is still very much Yorkshire Dales at heart.

Ribblesdale

Still on the western side, Ingleton and Settle are the centres for exploring the limestone uplands that drain into the Ribble and Lune. You can be forgiven for straying into Lancashire here, perhaps to pick off the shapely summit of Pendle Hill or explore the fringes of the Forest of Bowland which lines the western side of Ribblesdale. Here, too, you'll find the famous Devil's Bridge at Kirkby Lonsdale, a soaring medieval structure over the River Lune, with the dark heights of Barbon Fell as a brooding backdrop.

Wharfedale

Returning to indisputable Yorkshire, Wharfedale, with its origins high on the fells at Oughtershaw, cuts a curving U-shaped line between craggy tops and limestone side valleys, past Hubberholme, Kettlewell and Grassington, then the romantic ruins of the priory at Bolton Abbey. From here the scenery changes subtly, the valley widening between heather moorlands through elegant Ilkley and, after one last moorland flourish on Otley's Chevin, beyond into the plains. From the ancient stone circle near the top of Ilkley's famous moor you can see for over 50 miles (80km), perhaps picking out the Kilburn White Horse on the North York Moors or the tower of York Minster on a clear day.

Nidderdale

Beside the Wharfe runs Nidderdale, a quiet, unassuming valley with great reservoirs in its upper reaches. Left out of the Yorkshire Dales National Park, this tranquil corner of grouse moors, pastureland and scattered settlements is now protected by the Nidderdale Area of Outstanding

Using this Book

Information Panels

An information panel for each walk shows its relative difficulty (➤ 5), the distance and total amount of ascent (that is how much ascent you will accumulate throughout the walk). An indication of the gradients you will encounter is shown by the rating 🔺🔺🔺 (fairly flat ground with no steep slopes) to 🔺🔺🔺 (undulating terrain with several very steep slopes).

Minimum Time

The minimum time suggested is for approximate guidance only. It assumes reasonably fit walkers and doesn't allow for stops.

Suggested Maps

Each walk has a suggested map. This will usually be a 1:25,000 scale Ordnance Survey Explorer map. Laminated aqua3 versions of these maps are longer lasting and water resistant.

Start Points

The start of each walk is given as a six-figure grid reference prefixed by two letters indicating which 100km square of the National Grid it refers to. You'll find more information on grid references on most Ordnance Survey maps.

Dogs

We have tried to give dog owners useful advice about how dog friendly each walk is. Please respect other countryside users. Keep your dog under control at all times, especially around livestock, and obey local bylaws and other dog control notices. Remember it is against the law to let your dog foul in many public areas, especially in villages and towns.

Car Parking

Many of the car parks suggested are public, but occasionally you may find you have to park on the roadside or in a lay-by. Please be considerate when you leave your car, ensuring that access roads or gates are not blocked and that other vehicles can pass safely. Remember that pub car parks are private and should not be used unless you have the owner's permission.

Maps

Each walk is accompanied by a sketch map drawn from the Ordnance Survey map and appended with the author's local observations. The scale of these maps varies from walk to walk. Some routes have a suggested option in the same area with a brief outline of the possible route. You will need a current Ordnance Survey map to make the most of these suggestions.

Natural Beauty. Again the haunting remains of once flourishing lead mines punctuate the dramatic landscape, none more so than at Greenhow Hill, between Pateley Bridge and Grassington, where the history of the mines can be traced back to Roman times.

Airedale

Running parallel with the Wharfe glides the River Aire. Its source obscured by complex limestone cave systems around Malham Cove, it cuts through gentle glaciated countryside before finding its shape again on the fringes of West Yorkshire. Here it narrows and the distinctive dark stone has been shaped into countless mills and their attendant rows of workers' houses. Above them brood silent moors, where once the Brontë sisters found their inspiration. Most of the mills have long since ceased production and in Bingley and Haworth you will find charming mini-townscapes, where the industrial past blends into a picturesque present

Walking in Safety

All these walks are suitable for any reasonably fit person, but less experienced walkers should try the easier walks first. Route finding is usually straightforward, but you will find that an Ordnance Survey map is a useful addition to the route maps and descriptions.

Risks

Although each walk here has been researched with a view to minimising the risks to the walkers who follow its route, no walk in the countryside can be considered to be completely free from risk. Walking in the outdoors will always require a degree of common sense and judgement to ensure that it is as safe as possible.

- Be particularly careful on cliff paths and in upland terrain, where the consequences of a slip can be very serious.

- Remember to check tidal conditions before walking on the seashore.

- Some sections of route are by, or cross, busy roads. Take care and remember traffic is a danger even on minor country lanes.

- Be careful around farmyard machinery and livestock, especially if you have children with you.

- Be aware of the consequences of changes in the weather and check the forecast before you set out. Carry spare clothing and a torch if you are walking in the winter months. Remember the weather can change very quickly at any time of the year, and in moorland and heathland areas, mist and fog can make route finding much harder. Don't set out in these conditions unless you are confident of your navigation skills in poor visibility. In summer remember to take account of the heat and sun; wear a hat and carry spare water.

- On walks away from centres of population you should carry a whistle and survival bag. If you do have an accident requiring the emergency services, make a note of your position as accurately as possible and dial 999.

PUBLIC TRANSPORT ⓘ

Where the Dales run into Metropolitan West Yorkshire, you'll find the public transport network is superbly coordinated by Metro, the West Yorkshire Passenger Transport Executive. It is relatively cheap, trains and buses run well into the evening, there is through ticketing between operators and day passes are available. You can find out more from their website, www.wymetro.com, or call MetroLine on 0113 245 7676. In the more rural parts of the region and the Yorkshire Dales National Park, public transport is less plentiful and times may not be convenient for walking on the same day as travelling. However great strides have been made recently to improve the situation and there are now frequent buses in summer from the surrounding towns to the most popular walking areas. You can get timetable information on the internet at www.dalesbus.org. Arriva Northern operate passenger trains on the Settle-to-Carlisle line, which runs right across the middle of the area covered by this book. For more information call the national rail enquiry line on 08457 48 49 50, or check www.pti.org.uk on the internet.

of tumbling becks and woods bedecked with bluebells in the spring. You'll also catch a glimpse of the great Leeds and Liverpool Canal, snaking its tortuous route between the great conurbations which lie either side of the Pennines.

Calderdale

Last of all these dales comes Calderdale, winding down from the bleak moors above Todmorden through villages and towns once dominated by textile mills, but now softened and healed by time. The sheltered little wooded cloughs that line the main valley were once full of industry, but now you can walk around the valley of the Hebden Water and forget how close you are to the heart of urban West Yorkshire.

Legacy

Across this landscape have strode giants, poets, great writers and storytellers. But it is usually the humdrum workers we have to thank for the exhilarating opportunities to explore the region on foot. Miners trod their paths up the gills and beneath the crags to find lead and coal. Drovers ushered their cattle and sheep down the dales and over the fellsides on their way to the lucrative markets further south. Strings of ponies carried freight over passes and simple bridges to keep more populous regions in salt and wool. Mill workers hurried down stepped and paved tracks to work their shifts in the mill. This is the real legacy of the Dales, and their best kept secret. This book picks out 50 of the best routes for the walker in the footsteps of the great and the humble, there is no better way to explore the Yorkshire Dales.

A Riverside Circuit High in the Dales

A classic walk in Upper Swaledale from Keld to Muker along Kisdon Side, and back by the river.

•DISTANCE•	6 miles (9.7km)
•MINIMUM TIME•	2hrs 30min
•ASCENT / GRADIENT•	820ft (250m) ▲▲ ▲ ▲
•LEVEL OF DIFFICULTY•	👥 👥 👥
•PATHS•	Field and riverside paths and tracks, 10 stiles
•LANDSCAPE•	Hillside and valley, hay meadows, riverside and waterfall
•SUGGESTED MAP•	aqua3 OS Explorer OL30 Yorkshire Dales – Northern & Central
•START / FINISH•	Grid reference: NY 892012
•DOG FRIENDLINESS•	Dogs on leads (there are lots of sheep)
•PARKING•	Signed car park at west end of village near Park Lodge
•PUBLIC TOILETS•	Keld and Muker
•CONTRIBUTOR•	David Winpenny

BACKGROUND TO THE WALK

Keld – its name is the Old Norse word for a spring – is one of the most remote of Dales villages. Set at the head of Swaledale, its cluster of grey cottages is a centre for some of the most spectacular walks in North Yorkshire. This walk follows, for part of its way, the traditional route by which the dead of the upper Dales were taken the long distance for burial in Grinton churchyard. Leaving the village, the walk takes the Pennine Way as it follows the the Swale down to Muker. This is Kisdon Side, on the slopes of the conical hill known as Kisdon. It was formed at the end of the ice age; the Swale used to flow west of the hill but glacial debris blocked its course and forced it to the east, in its current bed.

Muker and the Mines

As the Pennine Way goes west, eventually to climb the slopes of Great Shunner Fell, the walk joins the Corpse Way and descends into Muker. It is worth taking some time to explore the village. Like many Swaledale settlements, it expanded in the 18th and 19th centuries because of local lead mining. The prominent Literary Institute was built for the mining community; though in a nice reverse of fortunes, when the new chapel came to be built in the 1930s, dressed stone taken from the ore hearths at the Old Gang Mine down the valley was used. The Anglican church, which eventually did away with the long journey to Grinton, dates from 1580.

Rocks and Crackpot

Beyond Muker, the walk passes through hay meadows and along the banks of the Swale. Both sandstone and limestone are found in this section; look out for the sandstone bed underlying the river. The limestone of the area is part of the thick Ten Fathom bed, one of the Yoredale series of sedimentary rocks. Where the valley of Swinner Gill crosses the path are the remains of a small smelt mill which served the nearby Beldi Hill and Swinner Gill Mines. As you ascend the hill beyond, the ruins of Crackpot Hall, a farmhouse long abandoned because of mining subsidence and changes in farming fortune, are to your right. Its name means 'Crows Pothole'.

As the track descends the valley side, the waterfall of Kisdon Force is below you on the Swale, and there are high overhanging crags on the opposite bank. Further along, you turn downhill to the footbridge over the river, beside East Gill Force. Like all the Dales falls, the volume of its water can vary wildly from the merest summer trickle to a raging winter torrent. Whatever its condition, the rocks around can be very slippery and you should take special care if you leave the path to get a better view.

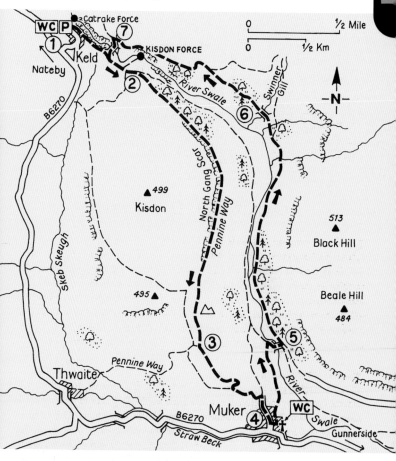

Walk 1 Directions

① Walk back down the car park entrance road, and straight ahead down the gravel track, signed 'Muker'. Continue along at the upper level, ignoring a path

downhill to the left. Go through a gate, pass a sign to **Kisdon Upper Force**, and continue along the track to a signpost.

② Turn right, following the **Pennine Way** National Trail. The path goes through a gated stone

Walk 1

stile, then through a gap in the wall to continue with a wall on your left. Go on through a gate and over four stiles to descend towards **Muker** to reach a signpost where the **Pennine Way** goes right.

③ Go straight on down the track, marked '**Muker**', between stone walls. Go through a wooden gate, still following the bridleway to **Muker**. The track becomes metalled, as it descends through two gates and into a walled lane in the village to a T-junction.

④ Turn left and left again by a sign to **Gunnerside and Keld**. Follow the paved path through five stiles to reach the river. Turn right and go over a stile to the footbridge.

⑤ Ascend the steps beyond the footbridge and turn left, signed '**Keld**'. Follow the course of the river along a clear track, until it curves right around **Swinner Gill**, over a footbridge by the remains of the lead workings, and through a wooden gate.

⑥ Go straight ahead up the hill and into woodland. The track eventually winds left then right round a stone barn, then downhill through a wooden gate to reach another gate above **Kisdon Force**.

⑦ Go left by a wooden seat, at a sign to **Keld**. Follow the stream down to a footbridge. Go through the gate and turn right, uphill, to a T-junction, where you turn right and follow the path back to the car.

WHILE YOU'RE THERE ⓘ
Take the minor road that leaves the B6270 just west of Keld to reach **Tan Hill** and its inn, the highest in England at 1,732 feet (528m) above sea level. With no neighbouring dwelling for at least 4 miles (6.4km) in any direction, it is as welcome a site for walkers today as it was for the packhorse-train drivers of the past, and the coal and lead miners who worked on the surrounding moors. It's not advisable to attempt the drive in fog, snow or icy weather.

WHAT TO LOOK FOR ⓘ
Around Muker traditional **hay meadows** are still to be found. They are an important part of the farmer's regime, which is why signs ask you to keep to single file as you walk through them. Such a method of farming helps maintain the wide variety of wild flowers that grow in the hay meadows. The barns, too, are part of older farming patterns, and form one of the most important visual assets of the Dales. The Muker area is especially rich in them – there are 60 within half a mile (800m) of the village. Their purpose was to store the hay after it was cut, to feed the three or four animals who would be over-wintered inside. This was to save the farmer moving stock and hauling loads of hay long distances. It also meant that the manure from the beasts could be used on the field just outside the barn.

Around Reeth in the Heart of Swaledale

Farmers, miners, knitters and nuns all played a role in the history of this part of Swaledale.

•DISTANCE•	5½ miles (8.8km)
•MINIMUM TIME•	2hrs
•ASCENT / GRADIENT•	508ft (155m) ▲▲▲
•LEVEL OF DIFFICULTY•	🚶 🚶 🚶
•PATHS•	Field and riverside paths, lanes and woodland, 14 stiles
•LANDSCAPE•	Junction of dales with field and surrounding moorland
•SUGGESTED MAP•	aqua3 OS Explorer OL30 Yorkshire Dales – Northern & Central
•START / FINISH•	Grid reference: SE 039993
•DOG FRIENDLINESS•	Dogs should be on leads for majority of walk
•PARKING•	In Reeth, behind fire station, or by the Green
•PUBLIC TOILETS•	Reeth, near Buck Hotel
•CONTRIBUTOR•	David Winpenny

BACKGROUND TO THE WALK

Reeth has always had a strategic role in the Yorkshire Dales. Set above the junction of Swaledale and Arkengarthdale on Mount Calva, it controlled the important route westwards from Richmond. Sheep were, for a long time, the basis of Reeth's prosperity – it has been a market town since 1695 – and there are still annual sheep sales each autumn, as well as the important Reeth Show around the beginning of September. The wool was used in Reeth's important knitting industry – both the men and women would click away with their needles at stockings and other garments. Reeth also used to be a centre for the lead mining industry, which extended up Arkengarthdale and over Marrick Moor.

Two Bridges and a Church

Reeth Bridge, reached by the Leyburn road from the Green, has suffered over the years from the effects of the swollen River Swale. The present bridge dates from the early 18th century, replacing one washed away in 1701, itself built after its predecessor succumbed in 1547. The path beside the river takes us to Grinton Bridge. Near by is Grinton church, once the centre of a huge parish that took in the whole of Swaledale, making very long journeys necessary for marriages and funerals. Curiously, it began life as a mission church for the Augustinian Canons of far-away Bridlington Priory on the east coast.

Nuns and Schools at Marrick

The approach to Marrick Priory along the lane suggests that you are about to reach one of the most important churches in the Dales. In a way that is true. Marrick in the Middle Ages was home to a group of Benedictine nuns. It was founded by Roger de Aske, whose descendent, Robert, was one of the leaders of the Pilgrimage of Grace, the uprising against King Henry VIII's closure of the monasteries. Hilda Prescott's novel *The Man on a Donkey,* about Robert Aske and the Pilgrimage, is partly set at Marrick. Today the nuns' buildings are partly demolished or absorbed into farm buildings. The church was reduced in size in 1811, and the complex is now used as a Youth Centre for the Diocese of Ripon and Leeds, offering outdoor sports and adventure training. After Marrick Priory the path climbs steeply uphill on rough stone steps called the Nun's Causey (a corruption of causeway). Now used as part of the Coast to Coast Walk, from St Bee's Head in Cumbria to Robin Hood's Bay on the east coast, this is said to be the route which the nuns from the priory built so they could reach the old Richmond road that ran along the summit of the hill. The original 365 steps have been broken up and removed over the centuries, but the path still retains a suitably medieval atmosphere.

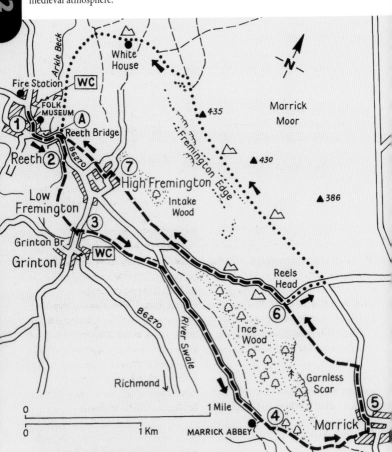

Walk 2 **Directions**

① From the **Green**, walk downhill, in the direction of Leyburn, to **Reeth Bridge**. Over the bridge, continue along the road as it swings right. About 100yds (91m) along, turn right at a footpath sign to **Grinton Bridge**.

② Follow the path through a gate and across fields to ascend steps and through a gate on to the bridge. Turn left, cross the road and take a track beside the bridge.

③ Follow the riverside path over four stiles, on to a metalled lane. Turn right and follow the lane to **Marrick Abbey**. Walk past the buildings, over a cattle grid, and turn left through a gate signed '**Marrick**'.

④ Walk up the grassy track, through a wooden gate and up the paved path through woodland. Go through a gate, up the path and through three more gates. Opposite **Harlands House** turn left up the metalled road, and left again at the T-junction.

WHERE TO EAT AND DRINK ⓘ
All three of Reeth's pubs – the **King's Arms** and the **Black Bull** (next door to each other) and the **Buck Inn** – provide good food at lunchtime and in the evenings. The Black Bull is particularly noted for its pies. There are also tea rooms and cafés around the Green.

⑤ Follow the road for ¼ mile (400m), and turn left over a stile at a footpath sign. Walk up the field, going right over a waymarked, gated stile and follow the wall, to go over another gated stile. Continue over a further stile by a metal gate, then through a second metal gate on to a road.

⑥ Turn left and follow the road for ¼ mile (1.2km). Where the road

WHILE YOU'RE THERE ⓘ
See the little **Swaledale Folk Museum** in Reeth, which has displays about life in the Dales. Lead mining and knitting, farming and religion, trades and professions, stone-walling and building are all shown through scenes of everyday toil. Alongside the exhibits are fascinating original photographs of Reeth and the Dales in the past.

bends left, turn right through a stile signed '**Fremington**'. Follow the path through fields, going through a gate, to another stile, then along a path to a lane.

⑦ Turn left. At the houses turn right, and as the lane bends left, go ahead to a stile by a gate. Keep by the wall on the left, and follow the path through four stiles back to **Reeth Bridge**. Cross the bridge and follow the road back to the **Green**.

Extending the Walk
You can extend this walk from Point ⑥ by turning right, up the lane, then left along a footpath which takes you on to the escarpment of **Fremington Edge**. After about 1¼ miles (2km) a path leads down to the left towards **White House**, from where you can descend into Arkengarthdale. Follow **Arkle Beck** to rejoin the main route at Point Ⓐ, near **Reeth Bridge** to return to **Reeth**.

WHAT TO LOOK FOR ⓘ
Traditionally Dales farmers had their own way of counting sheep, starting yahn, tayhn, tether, mether, mimp, hither, lither, anver, danver… and wherever you go in this area you'll come across the **Swaledale sheep**. This hardy breed, which spends much of its life on exposed moorland, has thick wool that is very resistant to wet. When spun it is hardwearing and modern treatment methods ensure that any harshness is removed. From the 16th century onwards Swaledale hand knitters used the wool in their products, particularly stockings. By the 18th century they were producing 18,000 pairs annually.

Leaden Arkengarthdale

Around an austere valley where hundreds of lead workers once toiled.

•DISTANCE•	8 miles (12.9km)
•MINIMUM TIME•	3hrs 15min
•ASCENT / GRADIENT•	1,213ft (370m) ▲▲▲
•LEVEL OF DIFFICULTY•	👫 👫 👫
•PATHS•	Mostly clear tracks, some heather moor, 4 stiles
•LANDSCAPE•	Mining-scarred moorland, with evocative remains of industry
•SUGGESTED MAP•	aqua3 OS Explorer OL30 Yorkshire Dales – Northern & Central
•START / FINISH•	Grid reference: NZ 005024
•DOG FRIENDLINESS•	Off lead for much of walk, except where sheep are present
•PARKING•	Pay-and-display car park at south end of Langthwaite village
•PUBLIC TOILETS•	None on route
•CONTRIBUTOR•	David Winpenny

BACKGROUND TO THE WALK

The quiet villages of Arkle Town and Langthwaite are grey clusters of houses in the austere splendour of Arkengarthdale. One of the most northerly of the valleys in the Dales, it runs northwards from Swaledale into dark moorland, with the battle-scarred Stainmore beyond its head. This isolation and stillness is deceptive, however, for until the beginning of the 20th century the surrounding hills were mined for lead. The metal was first dug here in prehistoric times, but industrial mining of the great veins of lead really began in the 17th century. By 1628 there was a smelt mill beside the Slei Gill, which you will pass on the walk, and it is possible to pick out the evidence of some of the early miners' methods.

Booze and Gunpowder

Booze (Norse for 'the house on the curved hillside') is now just a cluster of farm buildings, but was once a thriving mining community with more than 40 houses. Between Booze and Slei Gill you will pass the arched entrance to a level (a miners' tunnel) and behind it the remains of Tanner Rake Hush. This desolate valley is full of tumbled rock, left behind when the dammed stream at the top of the valley was allowed to rush down, exposing the lead veins. You'll pass the spoil heaps of Windegg Mines, before returning to the valley near Scar House, now a shooting lodge owned by the Duke of Norfolk but once belonging to the mine master. Near Eskeleth Bridge is the powder house, a small octagonal building, set safely by itself in a field. Built about 1804, it served the Octagon Smelt Mill, the remains of which can be traced near by. Just after you turn right along the road are the ruins of Langthwaite Smelt Mill. Lord of the Manor Charles Bathurst held the mining rights here for much of the 18th century. The CB Inn near the road junction is really the Charles Bathurst, in his honour.

Mining the west of the valley was more difficult than on the eastern side. This was an area known in the 19th century as the Hungry Hushes – the lead mined here was scarce and hard-won. The miners' tracks ascend the hill and eventually pass the junction of two long chimney flues. The walk then returns via Turf Moor into Langthwaite – it needs a feat of the imagination to visualise its heyday, peopled with hardened miners and their families.

Walk 3 Directions

① Leave the car park, turn right, then right again into **Langthwaite**. Go over the bridge and continue ahead between cottages. Climb the hill and follow the lane to the hamlet of **Booze**. Pass the farmhouse and a stone barn and follow the track to a gate.

② After the gate, where the track bends left, go straight on next to a broken wall. Bear right to go past a ruined cottage, then follow the path to the stream. Walk upstream, go through a gate and then cross the stream on stepping stones.

③ Walk slightly left, through the moorland, to reach a **wooden hut** near a crossing track. Turn left along the track. At a crossing of tracks go straight on, then at a T-junction turn left. Where the wall on your right ends, leave the track, bending right along a path and down to a gate in the corner of two walls.

> **WHERE TO EAT AND DRINK** ⓘ
> The **Red Lion** in Langthwaite has good beer and offers lunchtime bar food. The **CB Inn** further up the road is more upmarket, with a noted restaurant serving fine, fresh food – best to book for evening meals.

④ Follow the small gully downhill and go through a gate on to a track. Turn right along the track and continue through a gateway and on to another track by a barn. Follow this track as it bends left by a stone wall and then passes farm buildings. Go through two gates to reach a third, white gate.

⑤ Go through the white gate to enter the grounds of **Scar House**. Follow the drive as it bears right, downhill, go over a bridge and

> **WHILE YOU'RE THERE** ⓘ
> Continue up the road towards the head of Arkengarthdale and on to the 16th-century **Tan Hill Inn**, the highest pub in Britain at 1,732 feet (528m). Winters can last for six months here and ice, 4in (10cm) thick, has been known to form on the windows. The inn has hosted an annual sheep show on the last Thursday of May since 1951. Despite relying on a generator for its power, it boasts an award-winning website!

cattle grid at the bottom, then turn right. Follow the track to a road. Turn left, uphill, to a T-junction. Turn right and follow the road. After a cattle grid, turn left along a signed track.

⑥ At a gravelled area bear right and continue uphill on the track. Where it divides, go left beside spoil heaps and pass the junction of two flues. The track winds uphill, right then left, to reach a T-junction of tracks. Turn left and follow the track downhill to reach a road.

⑦ Turn left along the road. Just after a farmhouse turn right at a bridleway sign, which takes you towards the house; turn left before reaching it and follow the signed track. Go through a gate and continue downhill. Before a small **barn**, turn left. Go over four stiles to reach the road. Turn left back to the car park.

> **WHAT TO LOOK FOR** ⓘ
> **Dry-stone walls** are a typical feature of Arkengarthdale, as in much of the Yorkshire Dales. There are around 4,680 miles (7,530km) of such walls in the National Park, many of them built during the enclosure of former common land in the 17th to 19th centuries. These are the ones that head straight as an arrow for the fell tops. Earlier walls tend to enclose smaller fields and were built from rocks gathered from the fields – some may date from earlier than 1000 BC. They provide shelter for sheep and for smaller animals and birds, like whinchats. Many walls are derelict, and there are grants from various bodies available to farmers who want to repair them – a lack of skilled wallers is slowing down the work of repair.

Richmond's Drummer Boy

Following in the steps of the Richmond Drummer, to Easby Abbey.

•DISTANCE•	6 miles (9.7km)
•MINIMUM TIME•	2hrs 20min
•ASCENT / GRADIENT•	656ft (200m) ▲▲▲
•LEVEL OF DIFFICULTY•	🚶🚶🚶
•PATHS•	Field and riverside paths, a little town walking, 20 stiles
•LANDSCAPE•	Valley of River Swale and its steep banks
•SUGGESTED MAP•	aqua3 OS Explorer 304 Darlington & Richmond
•START / FINISH•	Grid reference: NZ 168012
•DOG FRIENDLINESS•	Dogs should be on leads for most of walk
•PARKING•	Friars Close long-stay car park
•PUBLIC TOILETS•	Friars Close car park and Round Howe car park
•CONTRIBUTOR•	David Winpenny

BACKGROUND TO THE WALK

The first part of the walk follows much of the route taken by the legendary Richmond Drummer Boy. At the end of the 18th century, the story says, soldiers in Richmond Castle discovered a tunnel that was thought to lead from there to Easby Abbey. They sent their drummer boy down it, beating his drum so they could follow from above ground. His route went under the Market Square and along to Frenchgate, then beside the river towards the abbey. At the spot now marked by the Drummer Boy Stone, the drumming stopped. The Drummer Boy was never seen again. Now the walk is re-enacted each year, with a local schoolboy playing the drum (but walking above ground!). The Green Howards Regimental Museum in the Market Square can tell you more about the drummer boy and his regiment.

Easby Abbey, whose remains are seen on your walk, was founded for Premonstratensian canons in 1155 by the Constable of Richmond Castle. Although not much of the church remains, some of the other buildings survive well, including the gatehouse, built about 1300. The refectory is also impressive, and you can see the infirmary, the chapter house and the dormitory. Just by the abbey ruins is the parish church, St Agatha's. It contains a replica of the Anglo-Saxon Easby Cross (the original is in the British Museum) and a set of medieval wall paintings showing Old Testament scenes of Adam and Eve, on the north wall, and the life of Jesus on the south, as well as depictions of activities such as pruning and hawking.

After the abbey, you'll cross the River Swale on the old railway bridge, and follow the trackbed for a while. This was part of the branch line from Richmond to Darlington, which opened in 1846. It was closed in 1970. The station, a little further along the Catterick Road, is now a garden centre, and the engine shed a gym. Look right over Richmond Bridge as you cross, to see how the stonework differs from one end to the other. It was built by two different contractors, one working for Richmond Council and one for the North Riding of Yorkshire. In the hillside below Billy Bank Wood, which you enter beyond the bridge, were copper mines dating back to the 15th century. After you have climbed the hill and crossed the 12 stiles (between Points ⑤ and ⑥), you're following the old route of the Swale, which thousands of years ago changed its course and formed the hill known as Round Howe.

Walk 4 Directions

① Leave the car park and turn right, then left at the T-junction. At the roundabout go left, then go right at the next roundabout down

Dundas Street, bending right into **Frenchgate** then left into **Station Road**. Just past the church, take **Lombards Wynd** left.

② Turn right at the next junction and follow the track, passing to the right of the **Drummer Boy Stone** along the path. Leaving Richmond behind, go over two stiles and follow the waymarks towards the **abbey** to another two stiles. Turn right along the track and right again, this time down the metalled lane which leads to the **abbey** in the village of **Easby**.

③ Go to the left of the car park along the track. Where it divides, keep on the higher path, then go right by **Platelayers Cottage** over the old railway bridge. Follow the track bed for 400yds (366m), and go left over a cattle grid, to follow the track right, to the road.

> **WHERE TO EAT AND DRINK** ⓘ
> Richmond has many places for food and drink. The **King's Head Hotel** in the Market Square has meals, sandwiches and afternoon teas. One of the places that locals recommend is the **Frenchgate Café**, with its bistro-like atmosphere.

④ Turn right, and follow the road for ½ mile (800m). Turn left up **Priory Villas**, bearing right to go in front of the houses and through three gates. Keeping parallel to the river, cross some playing fields and pass a clubhouse to a road.

⑤ Cross the road, and take a signed path opposite, to the left of the cottage. Climb steeply through the woodland, through a gate and a stile, bending right at the end of the woodland to a stile in a crossing fence. Turn right over the stile, and follow the signed path over 12 more

> **WHILE YOU'RE THERE** ⓘ
> Visit **Richmond Castle**, which looms over the Swale Valley through much of the walk. Its keep, more than 100ft (30m) high, was complete by 1180. Now in the care of English Heritage, the castle's central ward is surrounded by high curtain walls with towers. Inside the keep are unique drawings done in the First World War by conscientious objectors. They were imprisoned here in squalid conditions.

stiles. Just before reaching a gate, go right through a wall gap and left to another stile.

⑥ Turn right, to go through a gate. Follow the track as it bends downhill to a bridge. Cross it and walk to the lane. Go left and left again at the main road. After 200yds (183m) go right up a gravel track, to a junction.

⑦ Turn right, and follow the track uphill, bearing right then left near the farmhouse, to reach a metalled lane. Turn right and follow the lane back into **Richmond**. Go ahead at the main road and follow it as it bends left to the garage, where you turn left back to the car park.

Extending the Walk
You can extend this walk by continuing up the banks of the **River Swale**, along the track from Point ⑦, as far as Point Ⓐ. Return beneath the crags of **Whitcliffe Scar** to rejoin the main route about ½ mile (800m) further on at Point Ⓑ.

> **WHAT TO LOOK FOR** ⓘ
> **Wynds** are a feature of the Richmond townscape. A northern term, from the Old English word for 'to spiral', these narrow lanes usually link two wider streets. Just after the parish church you will turn left along Lombard's Wynd. This was once part of the ancient route up from the river to Frenchgate – 'Frankesgate' in the Middles Ages. Both these names suggest that this part of the town was once occupied by foreign workers.

Sedbergh and the Quakers

A gentle walk from Sedbergh to the Quaker hamlet of Brigflatts.

•DISTANCE•	4½ miles (7.2km)
•MINIMUM TIME•	1hr 30min
•ASCENT / GRADIENT•	131ft (40m)
•LEVEL OF DIFFICULTY•	
•PATHS•	Mostly on field and riverside paths, 7 stiles
•LANDSCAPE•	Playing fields give way to rich farmland, dominated by fells
•SUGGESTED MAP•	aqua3 OS Explorer OL19 Howgill Fells & Upper Eden Valley
•START / FINISH•	Grid reference: SD 659921
•DOG FRIENDLINESS•	Keep dogs on lead when animals in fields
•PARKING•	Pay-and-display car park just off Sedbergh main street (which is one-way, from west)
•PUBLIC TOILETS•	By car park
•CONTRIBUTOR•	David Winpenny

BACKGROUND TO THE WALK

The solid, stone-built town of Sedbergh, one of the largest settlements in the Yorkshire Dales National Park, was once in the West Riding of Yorkshire, but has been part of Cumbria since 1974. Two things – the Howgill Fells, especially the southernmost peaks of Winder and Crook, and Sedbergh School, which wraps itself around much of the town's south side – dominate this friendly town. Among its most notable old boys are the geologist Adam Sedgwick (► Walk 6) and the international rugby player Will Carling. Brilliant mathematician John Dawson taught Sedgwick and a group of other gifted scholars at the school in the late 18th century, and is commemorated with a bust by the sculptor Flaxman, high on the south nave wall in Sedbergh parish church. Almost opposite the church is the school's oldest building, built in 1716, now the school library.

The Quaker Link

The Sedbergh area is noted for its Quaker associations. In 1652 the founder of the Society of Friends, George Fox, came to the town and preached from a bench beneath a yew tree in the churchyard to a great crowd of people attending the Hiring Fair. On Firbank Fell, north west of Sedbergh, Fox again preached to a large crowd, this time from a large stone, still known as Fox's Pulpit. This meeting is said to mark the inception of the Society of Friends. Fox wrote, 'This was the place that I had seen a people coming forth in white raiment; and a mighty meeting there was and it is to this day near Sedbergh which I gathered in the name of Jesus.'

Meeting at Brigflatts

The best reminder of the early days of the Quakers in the area is to be found in the tiny hamlet of Brigflatts. Fox stayed here with Richard Robinson in a farmhouse in 1652, and in 1674 the Friends of the district decided to build a Meeting House. It still survives, and is the oldest in the North and the third oldest in England. From the outside it looks like a typical whitewashed cottage of the period, though, unlike most cottages, it had a stone roof from the start. Each winter the cracks in the slate were stuffed with moss to stop the rain getting in. George Fox was there in 1677, noting 'a great concourse...there were about 500/600 persons present. A very good meeting it was.' Around the beginning of the 18th century a schoolroom was built over the stable and the gallery was put up to accommodate the large gatherings. At the foot of the gallery stairs look out for the dog pen that was provided for the sheepdogs accompanying their masters to the meetings. Just up the lane from the Meeting House is the small and peaceful Burial Ground, first used in 1656.

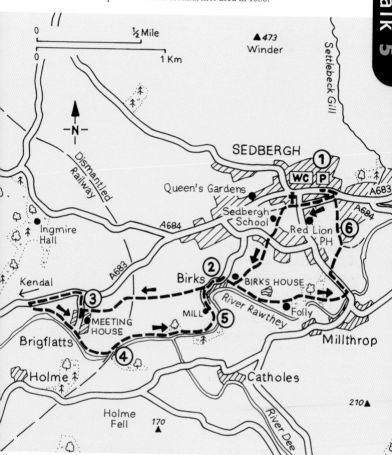

Walk 5 Directions

① From the car park, turn right along the main street, continue to the junction with the main road and turn left. At the churchyard turn right signed 'Cattle Market or Busk Lane'. At the next signpost, go left behind the pavilion, then straight ahead through two kissing gates and out on to a road. Cross and go through another metal kissing gate, signed 'Birks'. Follow the path through another gate to **Birks House**.

② Go through a kissing gate beyond the house and turn left along the lane. Opposite the **Old Barn** go right, through a metal kissing gate and follow the Brigflatts

Walk 5

sign roughly half left to a waymarker. Go through four gates and under the gated railway arch. Continue ahead and go through, in turn, a gate in a crossing wall, a metal kissing gate, and a farm gate on to a quiet lane opposite the **Quaker Burial Ground**.

③ Turn left to visit the **Meeting House**, then return to the gate, continuing on up the lane to the main road. Turn left. Just beyond the bend sign, go through a signed metal kissing gate in the hedge on the left. Follow the riverside path through two gates to another gate, to the left of a large railway bridge over the river.

④ Go through the gate and over the embankment to another gate. Continue along the riverside, passing through a gate near the confluence of two rivers, then two more gates to reach a metalled lane by an old **mill**.

⑤ Follow the lane back into **Birks**. Go right, though the kissing gate signed 'Rawthey Way' (you went through this gate the other way earlier in the walk). By the hedge around **Birks House**, bear right towards the river and over a stile. Follow the river to another stile, then climb slightly left to a stile by a gateway and then past a **folly**, to the

left of a wood, through a kissing gate. Walk through the wood to a stile. Cross the field to a metal gate then a stile on to a road by a bridge. Turn left. By the '30' sign, go right, though a stile. Cross the field to another stile, then bear left alongside the building to another kissing gate.

> **WHERE TO EAT AND DRINK** ⓘ
>
> Two of Sedbergh's pubs – the **Bull** and the **Dalesman** – offer meals at lunchtime and evenings, while the **Red Lion** has lunches (not Mondays). There are two cafés in the town, too; locals recommend the **Post Horn**, opposite the church.

⑥ Cross a drive to another kissing gate. Continue downhill to another, and go straight on along the lane to the main road. Cross the road and walk behind the row of houses, along **Sedbergh**'s main street to the car park.

> **WHILE YOU'RE THERE** ⓘ
>
> Spend a few quiet minutes in **Queen's Gardens** in Sedbergh. Described as 'a forgotten Victorian Park', the gardens are west of the town centre, just off the Kendal road. Presented to Sedbergh in 1906 by the splendidly named Mrs Upton-Cottrell-Dormer of Ingmire Hall in memory of Queen Victoria, there are shady trees and specially created glades for wildlife.

> **WHAT TO LOOK FOR** ⓘ
>
> The **Howgill Fells**, very different from the rest of the Yorkshire Dales, are huge, rounded humps of hills that seem to crowd in on each other like elephants at a watering hole. They are formed from pinkish sandstone and slates, 100 million years older than the limestone that underlies much of the rest of the National Park. The hills have few of the stone walls you will see elsewhere in the Dales – they are mostly common grazing land for the local farms and escaped the passion for enclosure in earlier centuries. One of the spectacular sights of the Dales, the great ribbon of waterfalls known as Cautley Spout is worth the drive from Sedbergh in the direction of Kirkby Stephen – park by the Cross Keys, a temperance inn. You can view the falls from there or walk part of the way towards it on a good path.

Adam Sedgwick's Dent

From the birthplace of a geologist, through the countryside that inspired him.

•DISTANCE•	6 miles (9.7km)
•MINIMUM TIME•	2hrs 15min
•ASCENT / GRADIENT•	918ft (100m) ▲ ▲ ▲
•LEVEL OF DIFFICULTY•	👫 👫 👫
•PATHS•	Tracks, field and riverside paths, some roads, 13 stiles
•LANDSCAPE•	Moorland and farmland, with wide views of Dentdale
•SUGGESTED MAP•	aqua3 OS Explorer OL2 Yorkshire Dales – Southern & Western
•START / FINISH•	Grid reference: SD 704871
•DOG FRIENDLINESS•	On lead in farmland and riverside section
•PARKING•	Pay-and-display car park at west end of Dent
•PUBLIC TOILETS•	At car park
•CONTRIBUTOR•	David Winpenny

BACKGROUND TO THE WALK

Dentdale is sometimes called 'the hidden valley'. Unlike most of the Yorkshire Dales it looks west towards the Lake District, and at its western end the limestone landscape gives way suddenly to the rounded Howgill Fells. It seems to have a milder climate and it is more thickly wooded, too. Its 'capital', Dent, is one of the most individual villages of the Dales. Its dog-legged main street is lined with stone cottages that front directly on to the cobbles, or cluster around the church. It is a fascinating spot to explore, with the added benefit of good pubs and tea-shops. It is also a busy place in the summer, with tourists and walkers attracted by the special feel of what comedian and walker Mike Harding has called 'the bonniest of all Dales villages'.

Man of the Rocks and the Terrible Knitters

Pride of place in the main street is a drinking fountain made from huge boulder of Shap granite and simply inscribed 'Adam Sedgwick 1785–1873'. It is a bold and simple memorial to Dent's most famous son. Sedgwick was born in the Old Parsonage by the village green; he was the son of the parson, and the surgeon who delivered him was, perhaps prophetically, another Dentdale genius, mathematician John Dawson. Sedgwick went to Sedbergh School and on to Cambridge, where his study of geology, inspired by the rocks of Dentdale, made him among the foremost authorities on the subject. He eventually became Professor of Geology at Cambridge – the university's fascinating geology museum is now named after him. He returned regularly to Dent, where his brother and his nephew both succeeded his father as vicar. 'Whenever I have revisited the hills and dales of my native country,' he wrote in 1866, when he was 81, 'I have felt a new swell of emotion, and said to myself, here is the land of my birth; this was the home of my boyhood, and is still the home of my heart.'

As well as farming, the other great industry of Dent, well into the 19th century, was knitting. 'The Terrible Knitters of Dent', the poet Southey called them – intending a compliment on their speed and industry. Men, women and children all knitted – often while engaged at other work. Adam Sedgwick remembered that 'with a speed that cheated the eye they went on with their respective tasks. Beautiful gloves were thrown off complete; and worsted stockings made good progress. There was no dreary noise of machinery; but there was the merry heart-cheering sound of the human tongue.' Dent's woollen socks kept the feet of the British Army warm while they fought Napoleon.

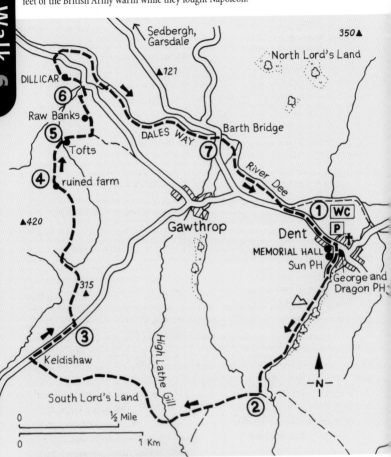

Walk 6 **Directions**

① Leave the car park and turn left, then right alongside the **Memorial Hall**. Pass the green and go straight on at the 'Flinter Gill' signpost. The metalled lane becomes a stony track and climbs steeply. Go over a stile by a gate and continue uphill, though a gate, to reach a wooden gate beside a seat. Go through the gate to a T-junction of tracks.

② Turn right, signed 'Keldishaw'. Follow the walled track for 1½ miles (2.4km), going through a gate and over a bridge over a stream, then downhill to a metalled road. Turn right and follow the road for ¼ mile (400m) to a signpost to Underwood on the left,

③ Go through the gate and follow the grassy track to a ladder stile, then continue with a wall on your left to reach a track. It bends right

WHERE TO EAT AND DRINK ℹ
Dent's two pubs – the much photographed **Sun** and the **George and Dragon** – both serve the excellent Dent Brewery beers and offer good food, as do the four tea rooms. The **Stone Close Café**, near the car park, also serves as a National Park information point.

and becomes a path on a ridge above the valley, eventually descending through the yard of a ruined **farmhouse**.

④ Bend right at the end of the farm buildings to follow a track to the right of a ruined stone wall. Go through a gap in a wall, then downhill, bending right to another gateway. After the gateway go straight ahead, away from the track, to a waymarked post. Turn left along the stream bank for a few paces, then go downhill to cross a simple bridge of two stones. Climb the other side of the bank and go through two gates by the buildings.

⑤ Continue down the farm track, until just before telephone lines, then cross it. Turn left by a tree and go through a waymarked gate. Walk ahead across the field and go round the right of the ruined farmhouse. Continue to wind downhill to a metal gate with a wooden hand gate beside it, after which the track bends right, descending to a metalled lane by a barn.

⑥ Turn left along the lane for a few paces and go straight ahead along the track to **Dillicar** farm. In the farmyard bear left then right down to a metal gate, then bear right again down to a ladder stile by a barn. Turn left along the lane, then right to a plank bridge and a stile signposted '**Dales Way**'. Cross the field to the river bank, then follow the river upstream, going through seven gates and over three footbridges to arrive at gated stone steps up to a squeeze stile and on to a stone bridge.

WHILE YOU'RE THERE ℹ
Visit the **Sedgwick Geological Trail** beside the A684 in neighbouring Garsdale, where you can find out more about Adam Sedgwick and his geological discoveries. The trail takes you into the valley of the Clough River and explains how the line of the Dent Fault, first identified by Sedgwick, can be traced by the marked differences of landscape. To the east is the typical Dales landscape of the Yoredale series of sedimentary rocks and to the west the much older Silurian rocks of the Howgill Fells – geologically part of the Lake District.

⑦ Cross the bridge, going through another stile and down steps, to continue along the riverside path. Go through four stiles and across a plank bridge, then through three more stiles to emerge on to a road. Turn left and follow the road back into **Dent**.

WHAT TO LOOK FOR ℹ
Just by the porch of Dent church is the gravestone of George Hodgson, said to have been the **Dent Vampire**. Born in 1621, George lived to the then astonishing age of 94. Idle Dentdale rumour, even during his lifetime, suggested that his longevity was the result of a pact that he had made with the Devil, and that his prominent canine teeth – probably the only ones left in his head by that time! – were used for sucking youthful blood from hapless victims. Hedging their bets, the Dent villagers gave him a churchyard burial – but in a remote corner. But when some of them claimed to have seen his spectre abroad, and that some unexplained deaths in the dale may have been attributed to it, they dug him up and reburied him, with a stake through his heart, by the porch.

Through Grisedale, 'The Dale that Died'

The derelict farmsteads of this once-thriving dale tell their story of hardship and surrender.

•DISTANCE•	5 miles (8km)
•MINIMUM TIME•	2hrs 15min
•ASCENT / GRADIENT•	722ft (220m) ▲▲ ▲▲ ▲
•LEVEL OF DIFFICULTY•	🚶🚶 🚶🚶 🚶🚶
•PATHS•	Moorland paths and tracks, may be boggy, 19 stiles
•LANDSCAPE•	Rough moors and hidden valleys, railway within earshot
•SUGGESTED MAP•	aqua3 OS Explorer OL19 Howgill Fells & Upper Eden Valley
•START / FINISH•	Grid reference: SD 786919
•DOG FRIENDLINESS•	Sheep on moorland – keep dogs under close control
•PARKING•	Roadside parking on road to Garsdale Station
•PUBLIC TOILETS•	None on route
•CONTRIBUTOR•	David Winpenny

BACKGROUND TO THE WALK

Whenever Grisedale is mentioned, it is tagged 'The Dale that Died'. This perhaps unfortunate label was the title of a television documentary made in the mid-1970s that followed the fortunes, and misfortunes, of families farming in this remote valley that pushes north from Garsdale towards the massive heights of Wild Boar Fell. The programme in particular dealt with a former miner, Joe Gibson, who struggled against the climate, misfortune and the lack of subsidies for upland farmers to try to make even a bare living from the land – a struggle that eventually proved unequal and ended with his retreat from Grisedale. The fields that Joe and his neighbours once tended have now reverted to moorland and scrub, and a plantation of conifers climbs the side of East Baugh Fell from the valley bottom. Nearly all the farmhouses are now derelict. At the head of the valley stands Round Ing, once a substantial building with barns and animal sheds. Now it has tumbled down, its walls diminishing in height every year. What remains of the plants and shrubs in its garden still bloom in summer, but, like West Scale and East Scale a little downstream, it is a place of sadness and lost hope.

From the Pigs to the Railway

Grisedale's earlier history is obscure – perhaps unsurprisingly for such a remote place. Its name comes from Old Norse and means the valley in which the pigs were kept, so the dale must have been farmed from its earliest days. In the Middle Ages it was owned by the monks of Jervaulx Abbey at the far end of Wensleydale; Grisedale is only about a mile (1.6km) from the River Ure as it begins its decent though Wensleydale. Grisedale seems to have been populated steadily throughout the later centuries, partly because it was adjacent to one of the main routes to the Lake District from the east – Wordsworth recommends it in his *Guide through the District of the Lakes* (1820). It also received a boost when the Settle-to-Carlisle railway arrived in 1876, and the connecting Wensleydale line in 1878.

After Round Ing, the walk passes the derelict barns of Flust, where it fords a stream, then continues to the inhabited farmsteads of Fea Fow and East House. It then crosses the ridge (and the county boundary between Cumbria and North Yorkshire) with views towards Ingleborough and Whernside, and descends through South Lunds Pasture to Grisedale Crossing on the Settle-to-Carlisle railway line. Beside a typical railway house is a metal footbridge across the line, put up in 1886 to replace an earlier wooden one. Here the line is just below its highest point, the 1,169 ft (356m) Ais Gill summit.

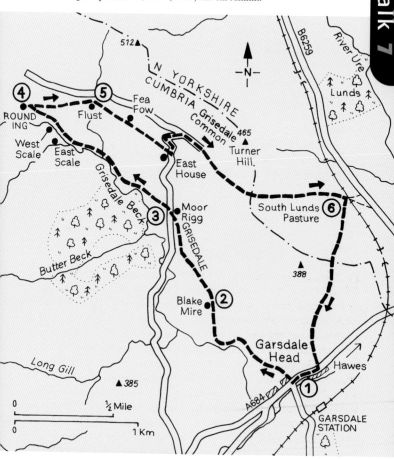

Walk 7 Directions

① Walk down the hill to the main road. Cross at the junction and take a stile signed 'Grisedale and Flust'. Bear gradually right to a stile in a wall. Follow the sign straight ahead on the track across the field to a signpost. Follow the sign to a gated stile, right of the farmhouse.

② Go half right after the stile, over two more stiles then downhill over a clapper bridge and on to a stile and signpost by a ruined building. Go over the stile and follow the sign, though a stile to the left of a barn and onwards to a signpost left of a white-painted farmhouse.

③ Cross the metalled lane to another signposted stile. After two

Walk 7

WHERE TO EAT AND DRINK ⓘ
The nearest place is the **Moorcock Inn** a mile (1.6km) east of Garsdale Station on the A684, at its junction with the B6259. It serves good beer (including Black Sheep bitter) and has hot meals both at lunchtime and in the evening.

more stiles, follow the wall towards a ruined building, descending to walk beside the stream. Go through a gate and bear right to a signposted stile. Continue with the steam on your left to a gate, then to a humpback bridge. Do not cross, but follow two signposts uphill and along the ridge, bearing slightly right to reach the tumbled farm buildings of **Round Ing**.

④ Follow the signpost at Round Ing towards **East House**. There is no clear path, but look for a waymarked post by the end of the wall. Continue towards houses on the hillside. Cross a stream. Continue downhill to a grassy track and turn left towards the barn. Just before it turn right, off the track, to pass below the barn to a gate. Go through the gate and bear right across the stream.

⑤ Pass a ruined building and head across the field towards the houses. Go over a wooden stile and then over a ladder stile right of the farm

buildings. Follow the track through two gates on to a metalled road. Turn left, uphill, to a T-junction, where the metalled road ends. Turn right, along the track, first following the wall on your right then continuing to a stile beside a gate. Walk downhill to railway buildings in the valley bottom.

WHILE YOU'RE THERE ⓘ
Visit **Garsdale Station**, which is the local station for Hawes 6 miles (9.7km) to the east. The station has the only fully-operating signal box on the Settle-to-Carlisle line, while just to the south the highest water troughs in the world were once located and trains at speed gathered water from them. The station was originally called Hawes Junction, became Hawes Junction and Garsdale in 1900 and just Garsdale in 1932. The Hawes line closed in 1959, though a group of local people is determined that it will reopen.

⑥ Go over a wooden stile by the buildings, pass the footbridge and, just by the track over the line, take a gated stile on the left corner. Walk half right, away from the railway, pass through a tumbled wall and follow the path over two stiles and through another broken wall to pass beside a barn and on to a stile on to the main road. Turn right, back to the road junction and the parking place.

WHAT TO LOOK FOR ⓘ
Red squirrels have been reported in Garsdale, and refuge sites are being established in conifer woodland to help protect and encourage them. You will be very lucky to spot one, but you may see the tell-tale signs of their presence in the nibbled and discarded pine cones in the woods. The animals are around 8in (20cm) long and their tails add another 7in (17cm). While their bodies are the characteristic rusty red – though in winter it turns more grey – their tails are often much paler in colour. There have been red squirrels in Britain since prehistoric times – unlike their larger grey relatives, which came from America in the 1870s, either escaping captivity or being deliberately introduced. Though the two types sometimes fight, the grey squirrel is more of an opportunist than an invader. Its spread seems to have coincided with a disease that drastically reduced the number of reds in Britain, letting the greys take over the reds' traditional areas.

Hawes and Hardraw

From busy Hawes to Hardraw, with a visit to the famous waterfall.

•DISTANCE•	5 miles (8km)
•MINIMUM TIME•	2hrs
•ASCENT / GRADIENT•	426ft (130m) ▲ ▲ ▲
•LEVEL OF DIFFICULTY•	🚶 🚶 🚶
•PATHS•	Field and moorland paths, may be muddy, 44 stiles
•LANDSCAPE•	Moorland and farmland
•SUGGESTED MAP•	aqua3 OS Explorer OL30 Yorkshire Dales – Northern & Central
•START / FINISH•	Grid reference: SD 870898
•DOG FRIENDLINESS•	Dogs under close control throughout; lots of stiles
•PARKING•	Pay-and-display car park off Gayle Lane at west of Hawes
•PUBLIC TOILETS•	At car park
•CONTRIBUTOR•	David Winpenny

BACKGROUND TO THE WALK

For many people, Hawes means two things – Wensleydale cheese and motorcyclists. The bikers use the town as a base at summer weekends and bank holidays, enjoying a friendly drink in the pubs and spectacular rides on the surrounding roads. However, it is the Wensleydale Creamery that attracts other visitors. Just above the car park in Gayle Lane, the Creamery offers tours and tastings, as well as the chance to buy a traditional Wensleydale.

Cheese has been made in Wensleydale since French monks brought the skill here in 1150. After centuries of farm production, a factory was started in Hawes in 1897. It was saved from closure in the 1930s by local man Kit Calvert, and again in 1992, when the local managers bought the creamery from Dairy Crest. It is now a thriving business and a vital part of the Hawes economy.

Force of Nature

The walk gives you the chance – which you should take – to visit the famous Hardraw Force, a 90ft (27m) waterfall in a deep and narrow valley. There is a modest entrance charge, payable in the Green Dragon pub in Hardraw village, and a short, pleasant walk to the fall. Despite appearances, what you see isn't entirely natural. On 12 July 1889 an unprecedented deluge on the hill above caused a wall of water to descend Hardraw Beck and through the valley, destroying buildings in the village and washing away bridges. It also devastated the waterfall, reducing it to a mudslide. After seeing to the clearing up in the village and the welfare of his tenants, the local landowner, Lord Wharncliffe, arranged for his workmen to reconstruct the lip of the fall, pinning together the blocks of shattered stone. This he did so successfully that today's visitors have no idea of the disaster that happened more than a century ago.

Bands in the Valley

On the way to and from Hardraw Force you will pass the circular bandstand for the annual Hardraw Scar Brass Band Contest, usually held in September. It was founded in 1881, and is reputed to be the second oldest brass band competition in the world. Bands from throughout the North of England – and beyond – compete in the championship, cheered on by supporters who crowd the valley floor and hillsides of this natural amphitheatre.

Old Ropes – and New

From the tiny village of Sedbusk, near the end of the walk, came the area's first-known rope maker, John Brenkley, who died in 1725. The tradition is continued today in Hawes by W R Outhwaite and Son in their Hawes Ropeworks. Visitors can see work in progress on ropes of all types, including ropes for bells, barriers and banisters, as well as dog leads and braids.

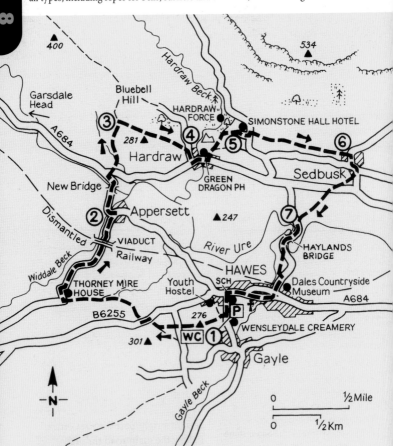

Walk 8 Directions

① From the car park turn left, then go right over a stile signed 'Youth Hostel'. Follow a track, bending uphill to a stile. Pass a barn, cross six stiles and a lane, to a road. Turn left then right through a gate signed

'Thorney Mire House'. Follow the path for ½ mile (800m) to a gate on to a lane. Turn right. Follow this for ¾ mile (1.2km), passing under the **viaduct** to the road at **Appersett**.

② Turn left across the bridge. Follow the road and cross the next bridge, then bend left to the

Walk 8

junction. Go through a stile, signed 'Bluebell Hill'. Cross the field, go through a gate and over a bridge, then bear half left uphill. Go through a gate and continue to a crossroads signpost.

③ Turn right and follow the valley to a stile (**Bob's Stile**). Cross the field beyond, go over a stile then turn left to a ladder stile over a wall. Cross the field towards **Hardraw**, going over wooden stile, then over a ladder stile into a lane.

④ Turn right then left at the main road and cross the bridge. **Hardraw Force** entrance is through the **Green Dragon** pub. Immediately

beyond the pub, turn left and go right through a signed gap in the wall, through a courtyard and over a stile. Follow the flagged path over another stile, steeply uphill, over a stile and up steps. By the house, go through a stile and right of the stables, then through two more stiles on to a lane by the **Simonstone Hall Hotel**.

⑤ Turn right then left along the road. Almost immediately turn right though a stile signed 'Sedbusk'. Follow the track through a metal gate and over two ladder stiles and another gateway then through 14 stiles into **Sedbusk**.

⑥ Turn right along the road, bend left near the post-box and go downhill. Go right, over a stile signed 'Haylands Bridge'. Cross the field, bend right to a stile in a crossing wall, then down to a stile on to a road. Cross to another stile and follow the path, cross a stream, go over a stile then bear right over a humpback bridge. Go through a gated stile on to a road.

⑦ Turn left. Cross **Haylands Bridge** and beyond go right through a kissing gate signed 'Hawes'. Follow the path, go over a stile, then turn left, then right on to the main road. At the junction cross and turn right past the post office. Follow the main road through **Hawes**, turning left after the school to the car park.

Cowgill, a Geologist and the River Dee

An easy walk at the head of Dentdale, in the footsteps of Adam Sedgwick, beside the River Dee and back through farmland.

•DISTANCE•	3½ miles (5.7km)
•MINIMUM TIME•	1hr 30min
•ASCENT / GRADIENT•	131ft (40m)
•LEVEL OF DIFFICULTY•	
•PATHS•	Tracks, field and riverside paths, some roads, 17 stiles
•LANDSCAPE•	Lush valley bottom, views of the fells and farmland
•SUGGESTED MAP•	aqua3 OS Explorer OL2 Yorkshire Dales – Southern & Western
•START / FINISH•	Grid reference: SD 742864
•DOG FRIENDLINESS•	Keep under close control; lots of stiles
•PARKING•	Parking place at Ibbeth Peril
•PUBLIC TOILETS•	None on route
•CONTRIBUTOR•	David Winpenny

BACKGROUND TO THE WALK

Cowgill, near the narrow head of Dentdale, is a cluster of houses alongside the River Dee. Now mostly an agricultural, holiday and residential settlement, in the past it housed both miners and mill workers – near Ewegales Bridge was Dee Mill, where worsteds were spun at the beginning of the 19th century. The fast-flowing Dee, which may be named after a Celtic river goddess, and in turn gives its name to Dentdale, provided the motive power; it tumbles and slides across limestone terraces and through gorges on its way to join the River Rawthey near Sedbergh. Though innocent in good weather, the river can be fierce after rain – in 1870 Ewegales Bridge and Lea Yeat Bridge, both on the walk, were swept away.

Perilous Undertaking

The start of the walk crosses a footbridge over the river as it rushes through a gorge where there is a waterfall called Ibbeth Peril. The waterfall has a cave (reputedly the home of a witch called Ibby) behind it – just one of a series of caves and passages that riddle the limestone in this part of the dale. Much favoured by speleologists, access to the main system (for the experienced only) is through a narrow entrance in the riverbank, which leads to a passage eventually opening into a large cavern. There are other caverns and underground waterfalls beyond, though the whole system has yet to be explored in full.

The Queen Intervenes

St John's Church at Cowgill, seen across the river near Ewegales Bridge, owes much to geologist Adam Sedgwick (▶ Walk 6). His sister started a Sunday school in Cowgill at the beginning of the 19th century, and by the 1830s there was a pressing need for a church. Sedgwick himself laid the foundation stone in 1837, when a crowd of 700 gathered in celebration. 'I handled the trowel,' he later wrote, 'and laid the stone, then addressed my countrymen, after which we again uncurled ourselves into a long string to the tune of God Save the King and the strangers, school children, and some others went down to Dent and had cold meat and coffee at the old parsonage. My sister made thirty-six gallons of coffee in a brewing vessel.' The early days of the chapel were not straightforward; diocesan officials first failed to register it as a place of worship at all, then called it by the wrong name. It took the personal intervention of Queen Victoria – Sedgwick had been a close acquaintance of Prince Albert – to sort out the mess.

Walk 9

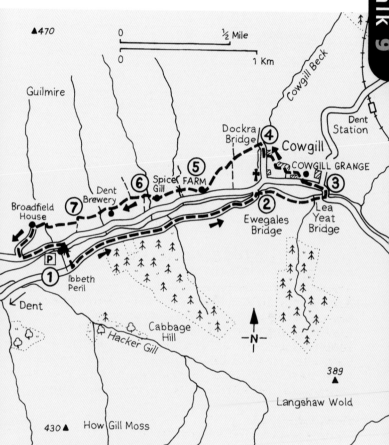

Walk 9 Directions

① Leave the back of the car park on a footpath going through woodland. Cross over a footbridge, then head across the field to a gate and turn left along the road. Follow the road for 1 mile (1.6km) until you get to a stone bridge over the **River Dee**.

② Don't cross the bridge, but continue along the riverside over a stile signed 'Lea Yeat'. Go through a stone stile and across two tributary streams, to a wooden stile on to **Lea Yeat Bridge**. Cross the bridge, then turn left at the signpost towards Dent and Sedbergh.

③ Just beyond the postbox on the left, follow a sign on the right to

Dockra Bridge. Go a short way up the drive for **Cowgill Grange**, then bear left to a gated stile. Go ahead, passing through two gates in front of a cottage and on to a track. Bear right. The path goes round the left end of two houses, through three gates and a stile. After the last gate, turn left to reach a track and go right to **Dockra Bridge**.

WHILE YOU'RE THERE

Visit **Dent Brewery**, which you pass on the walk at Hollins. It is not open to casual visitors – so don't just drop in – but visits are available every Saturday, starting from the George and Dragon in Dent, with transport to the brewery. You can sample some of the Brewery's prize-winning beers, many with sheep-related names such as Sheep and Shearful, Baarister and Ewe are the Weakest Link.

④ Cross the bridge, bend right then take a stile on your left. Go half left to a stile in a crossing wall. Continue ahead to a waymarked hand gate. Go right of the barn, though a gateway in a crossing wall to another gated stone stile, then half left across the field towards the **farmhouse** to a signposted stile.

⑤ After the stile, go half right, then through another stile. Continue to another stile, then head towards farm buildings, go over a stone stile

by a gateway beside the barn and through another gate. Pass the farmhouse, bend right and then left behind a barn to a bridge with steps and a gated stile beyond.

⑥ Cross the field to another stile. Just beyond, turn right along a track. As it bends right, go ahead to pass a house, through a gate and behind another building to a wooden stile. Go ahead across the field to a stone stile, go left of the barn on to a track over a stream and uphill again.

⑦ Curve round the left of the next barn and follow the wall. At the next farm buildings, go through a metal gate by a barn, then follow the walled lane right. After another gate bear left, through a stile, go to the right of the farm building and on to a track. Turn right, bear left through a waymarked gate, pass the farmhouse and follow the track to the road. Turn left to return to the car park.

WHERE TO EAT AND DRINK

There is nowhere immediately on the route, so head for Dent, with its two pubs and four tea rooms, or go east towards Dent Head viaduct for the **Sportsman's Inn**, which serves bar meals. It is usually closed in the afternoons.

WHAT TO LOOK FOR

While on the first, eastward, part of the walk look up to the facing hillside to see the white-painted Victorian buildings of **Dent Station** – the highest mainline railway station in England. It is 1,132ft (345m) above sea level and is one of the stops on the spectacular Settle-to-Carlisle line. While it can be an inhospitable place when the winds blow and the winter storms set in, it proved a way into the wider world for the people of Dentdale – even though to reach it from Dent meant a 4-mile (6.4km) walk and a stiff climb. In the later part of his life it was the route regularly taken by Adam Sedgwick (► Walk 6) on his way to and from York to reach London or Cambridge. It is still used by local people today – you may see them walking along the valley roads carrying their supermarket shopping from Settle or Carlisle. And you will certainly hear the whistle of the trains as they pass over Dent Head and Arten Gill viaducts as they approach Dent Station.

Semerwater – a Legendary Glacial Lake

Legends – perhaps with a basis in dim and distant truth – surround Yorkshire's biggest natural lake.

•DISTANCE•	5 miles (8km)
•MINIMUM TIME•	2hrs
•ASCENT / GRADIENT•	853ft (260m) ▲▲▲
•LEVEL OF DIFFICULTY•	🚶🚶🚶
•PATHS•	Field paths and tracks, steep ascent from Marsett, 19 stiles
•LANDSCAPE•	Valley, lake and fine views over Wensleydale
•SUGGESTED MAP•	aqua3 OS Explorer OL30 Yorkshire Dales – Northern & Central
•START / FINISH•	Grid reference: SD 921875
•DOG FRIENDLINESS•	Dogs should be on leads
•PARKING•	Car park at the north end of the lake
•PUBLIC TOILETS•	None on route
•CONTRIBUTOR•	David Winpenny

BACKGROUND TO THE WALK

Semerwater was formed as the result of the end of the last ice age. Glacial meltwater attempted to drain away down the valley the glacier had gouged out of the limestone, but was prevented from doing so by a wall of boulder clay, dumped by the glacier itself, across the valley's end. So the water built up, forming a lake which once stretched 3 miles (4.8km) up Raydale. Natural silting has gradually filled the upper part of the lake bed, leaving Semerwater – at half a mile (800m) long Yorkshire's largest natural lake.

Legendary Semerwater

Semerwater boasts several legends. One concerns the three huge blocks of limestone deposited by the departing glacier at the water's edge at the north end. Called the Carlow Stone and the Mermaid Stones, they are said to have landed here when the Devil and a giant who lived on Addlebrough, the prominent hill a mile (1.6km) to the east, began lobbing missiles at each other. More famous is the story of the beggar who came to the town that once stood where the lake is now. He went from door to door, asking for food and drink, but was refused by everyone – except the poorest couple. Revealing himself as an angel, he raised his staff over the town, crying 'Semerwater rise, Semerwater sink, And swallow all save this little house, That gave me meat and drink.' The waters overwhelmed the town, leaving the poor people's cottage on the brink of the new lake. Some say the church bells can still be heard ringing beneath the waters.

There are indeed the remains of an ancient settlement beneath Semerwater. Houses perched on wooden stilts were built along the water's edge in Iron Age times, though there may have been an earlier settlement here in neolithic times, too, for several flint arrow heads have been found. A Bronze-Age spear head was also found, in 1937, when the lake's waters were lowered.

Setts and Quakers

Marsett, at the lake's southern end, and Countersett, to the north, both end with the Old Norse word denoting a place of hill pasture. Marsett is a hamlet of old farmhouses, and on the road to Countersett, at Carr End, is the house where Dr Fothergill was born in 1712. A famous Quaker philanthropist, he founded the Quaker school at Ackworth in South Yorkshire. The American statesman Benjamin Franklin said he found it hard to believe that any better man than Fothergill had ever lived. Countersett has one of several old Friends' Meeting Houses in Wensleydale, and the Hall was home, in the 17th century, to Richard Robinson, who was responsible for the spread of Quakerism in the Dales.

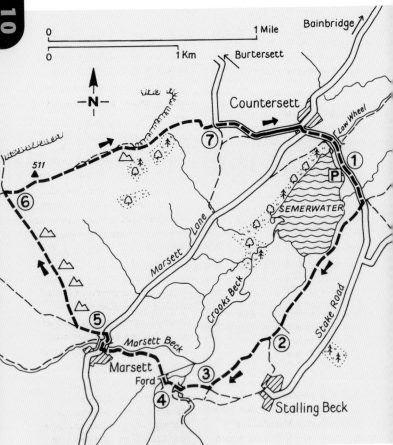

Walk 10 **Directions**

① Turn right out of the car park up the road. Opposite farm buildings go right over a ladder stile, signed 'Stalling Busk'. Go through a gated stile and ahead towards the barn, then through two stone stiles. Just beyond the second is a Wildlife Trust sign. Continue over two more stiles to a gate.

② Just beyond the gate, follow the **Marsett** sign to the corner of the field and over a gated stone stile. Follow the waymarked path as it curves beside the river, to a barn.

Go over a stile above the barn to another stile. Cross the field to another stile and on towards another barn, and on further to cross a stream bed.

③ Immediately afterwards, turn right down the well-worn footpath, which curves towards a roofless barn. Cross another three stiles, then turn right, following a path to the trees, with a stone wall on your right. Continue over two stiles to a footbridge and go straight on to a track, where you turn right to reach a ford.

WHAT TO LOOK FOR ⓘ
Semerwater offers a wide variety of habitats for wildlife. The waters of the lake, which have a high plankton content, support many fish including bream and perch, as well as crayfish. Water birds include great crested grebe and tufted duck. You may also occasionally see Whooper swans. Over the fringes of the lake dragonflies and damsel flies can be seen glittering in the summer. On the wet margins of the lake grow flowers such as marsh marigold, marsh cinquefoil, ragged robin and valerian, while in the dryer areas the wood anemone is frequently found. Birds such as lapwings, redshank and reed bunting may also be seen, while summer visitors include the sandmartin.

④ Before the ford, veer left over a footbridge and back on to the track, which winds into **Marsett**. Just before the village, follow the stream as it goes right, and make for the road by the red telephone box. Turn right over the bridge. 100yds (91m) beyond take a track signed '**Burtersett and Hawes**' (not the path by the river).

WHILE YOU'RE THERE ⓘ
Visit **Bainbridge**, with its wide green and attractive houses. The Romans had a fort here, Virosidum, on top of the hill called Brough. The River Bain, crossed by the bridge which gives the village its name, is England's shortest river, running all of 2 miles (3.2km) from Semerwater to the River Ure.

⑤ Walk uphill to a gate on the right at the start of the stone wall. Go over the stile and continue uphill, over three stiles. Soon after the steep path flattens out, you reach a track that crosses the path, coming through a gap in the wall on your left.

⑥ Turn right along the track, which goes through a gate in a wall. Where it divides, take the right fork downhill to a stile. The path descends steeply through two gates, to reach a crossing track. Continue straight ahead and follow the track as it bends left to a gate on to a metalled road.

⑦ Turn right and follow the road downhill to the staggered crossroads, turning right, then left, signed '**Stalling Busk**'. Go down the hill, over the bridge and back to the car park.

WHERE TO EAT AND DRINK ⓘ
The nearest place to Semerwater is Bainbridge, where the **Rose and Crown Hotel** by the Green dates back more than 500 years. The Bainbridge Horn, blown to guide travellers to the village in the dark winter months, hangs here. The hotel serves home-cooked local produce both in the bars and, in the evening, in the Dales Room Restaurant.

Villages, Falls and Intriguing Follies

From West Burton to Aysgarth and back, via the famous Aysgarth Falls.

•DISTANCE•	4 miles (6.4km)
•MINIMUM TIME•	1hr 30min
•ASCENT / GRADIENT•	394ft (120m) ▲ ▲ ▲
•LEVEL OF DIFFICULTY•	🏃 🏃 🏃
•PATHS•	Field and riverside paths and tracks, 35 stiles
•LANDSCAPE•	Two typical Dales villages, fields and falls on the River Ure
•SUGGESTED MAP•	aqua3 OS Explorer OL30 Yorkshire Dales – Northern & Central
•START / FINISH•	Grid reference: SE 017867
•DOG FRIENDLINESS•	Dogs should be on leads
•PARKING•	Centre of West Burton, by (but not on) the Green
•PUBLIC TOILETS•	None on route; Aysgarth National Park visitor centre is close
•CONTRIBUTOR•	David Winpenny

BACKGROUND TO THE WALK

Many people regard West Burton as the prettiest village in the Dales. Its wide, irregular green, with a fat obelisk of 1820, is surrounded by small stone cottages, formerly homes to the quarrymen and miners of the district – but no church. Villagers had to make the trek to Aysgarth for services. West Burton has always been an important centre. It is at the entrance to Bishopdale, with its road link to Wharfedale. South is the road to Walden Head, now a dead end for motorists, but for walkers an alternative route to Starbotton and Kettlewell. At the end of the walk you'll travel for a short time, near Flanders Hall, along Morpeth Gate, the old packhorse route to Middleham.

Two Halves of Aysgarth

After crossing the wide flood plain of Bishopdale Beck, and crossing Eshington Bridge, you climb across the hill to descend into Aysgarth. A village of two halves, the larger part, which you come to first, is set along the main A684 road. The walk takes you along the traditional field path from this part of the village to its other half, set around St Andrew's Church. It's worth looking inside; it contains the spectacular choir screen brought here from Jervaulx Abbey, down the dale, when it was closed by Henry VIII. Like the elaborate stall beside it, it was carved by the renowned Ripon workshops.

The Falls and the Wood

Beyond the church, the path follows the river beside Aysgarth's Middle and Lower Falls. The falls were formed by the Ure eating away at the underlying limestone as it descends from Upper Wensleydale to join the deeper Bishopdale. They are now one of the most popular tourist sights in the Yorkshire Dales National Park and the Upper Falls, by the bridge, featured in the film *Robin Hood, Prince of Thieves*. Robin (Kevin Costner) fought Little John here with long staves.

Mrs Sykes' Follies

On the return leg of the walk, you pass two oddities in the parkland behind the house at Sorrellsykes Park. These two follies were built in the 18th century by Mrs Sykes and no one seems to knows why. One is a round tower, with a narrowing waist like a diabolo. The other, sitting like Thunderbird 3 ready for lift-off, is known to local people as the 'Rocket Ship'. It is of no practical use, except for minimal shelter in the square room in its base, but it is just one of many folly cones throughout Britain. None of the others, however, have this elaborate arrangement of fins – presumably added because the builder had doubts about its stability.

Walk 11

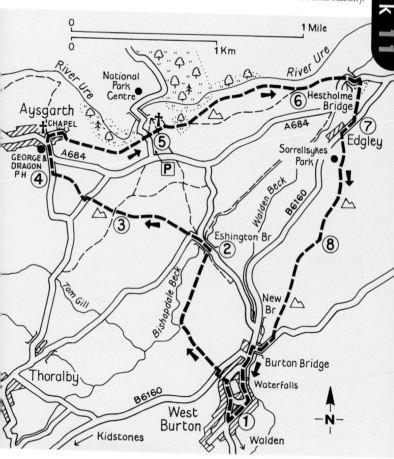

Walk 11 Directions

① Leave the **Green** near the Village Shop. Opposite '**Meadowcroft**' go left, signed '**Eshington Bridge**'. Cross the road, turn right then left, through a gate and down steps. Pass the barn, go through a gateway and across the field. Go through a gap

in the wall with a stile beyond, then bend right to a stile on to the road.

②Turn left, go over the bridge and ahead up the narrow lane. As it bends left go ahead through a stile, signed '**Aysgarth**', then on through a gated stile. Go ahead to a gap in the fence near a barn, then through a gate. Bend left to a gate in the field corner, go through a gateway and on to a stile. Turn right and descend to a signpost.

③ Go ahead to a stile in the field corner. Follow the signpost uphill to a gateway and go through a stile on the right. Cross the field half left to go through a gated stile on to a lane. Turn left, then almost immediately right through a stile, signed '**Aysgarth**'. Go through three stiles to a road.

WHAT TO LOOK FOR ⓘ

The woods around Aysgarth have long been used for the production of hazel poles, and there is evidence of this trade on the walk, with the now-overgrown stumps of the hazel trees sprouting many branches, some of them of considerable age. In Freeholders' Wood beside the Middle and Lower Falls, on the opposite side of the River Ure from the route of the walk, the National Park Authority has restarted this ancient craft of coppicing. The name comes from the French *couper*, meaning to cut. Each year the hazel trees are cut back to a stump – called a stool – from which new shoots are allowed to grow. As long as they are protected from grazing cattle, the shoots develop into poles, and can be harvested after around seven years' growth. Hazel poles are traditionally used for making woven hurdles, and the thinner stems for basket-weaving.

---

④ Turn right into the village, past the **George and Dragon**. At the left bend, go ahead toward the chapel, then right at the green, and follow the lane. Go through a stile by **Field House** and to another stile, turning left along the track. Follow the path through eight stiles to the road.

⑤ Go ahead into the churchyard, pass right of the church and go through two stiles, through woodland, then over another stile.

WHILE YOU'RE THERE ⓘ

Visit the **Yorkshire Carriage Museum** by the bridge below the church in Aysgarth. Housed in a former cotton mill that wove cloth for Garibaldi's 'Red Shirts', the revolutionary army of 19th-century Italy, the museum has a fascinating display of old-time transport, from carriages and carts to hearses and fire engines.

Follow the path down towards the river, descending steps to a gate, then a stile. When the path reaches the riverbank, take a stile right.

⑥ Follow the path over two stiles to a signpost, bending right across the field to a road. Turn left over the bridge, turning right into woodland a few paces beyond, signed '**Edgley**'. Go over a stile and cross the field to a gate on to the road.

⑦ Turn right. About 150yds (137m) along, go left over a stile, signed '**Flanders Hall**'. Walk below the follies on the ridge to a footpath sign, cross a track and go uphill to a stile with steps to it.

⑧ Opposite a stone barn go right, through a gate, and go downhill through two more gates, then over three stiles to a lane. Turn right and go over a bridge to join the village road. Turn left, back to the **Green**.

WHERE TO EAT AND DRINK ⓘ

In Aysgarth the **George and Dragon** is a good family pub serving meals. Up the road from the church, just off the route of the walk, **Palmer Flatt Hotel** has bar meals and a restaurant, as well as a beer garden with distant views. In West Burton, the **Fox and Hounds** is a traditional village pub serving meals. **Aysgarth Falls National Park Centre**, across the river from the church, has a good coffee shop.

A Kingdom for a Horse

From Middleham Castle, favourite home of King Richard III, and back via the gallops for today's thoroughbreds.

•DISTANCE•	7 miles (11.3km)
•MINIMUM TIME•	2hrs 30min
•ASCENT / GRADIENT•	475ft (145m) ▲ ▲ ▲
•LEVEL OF DIFFICULTY•	🚶 🚶 🚶
•PATHS•	Field paths and tracks, with some road walking, 18 stiles
•LANDSCAPE•	Gentle farmland, riverside paths, views of Wensleydale
•SUGGESTED MAP•	aqua3 OS Explorer OL30 Yorkshire Dales – Northern & Central
•START / FINISH•	Grid reference: SE 127877
•DOG FRIENDLINESS•	Livestock and horses in fields, so dogs on leads
•PARKING•	In square in centre of Middleham
•PUBLIC TOILETS•	Middleham
•CONTRIBUTOR•	David Winpenny

BACKGROUND TO THE WALK

When Richard III died at the Battle of Bosworth Field in 1485, Middleham lost one of its favourite residents. Richard had lived here, in the household of the Earl of Warwick – The Kingmaker – when a boy, and set up home here with the Earl's daughter Anne after their marriage. As Duke of Gloucester, it was his power base as effective ruler of the North under his brother Edward IV. Locals don't believe the propagandist version of Richard, promoted by Shakespeare's play, that he was a murderer – the Lord Mayor of York reported to his council after Bosworth that 'King Richard, late lawfully reigning over us, was through great treason piteously slain and murdered'. Middleham Castle today is a splendid ruin, with one of the biggest keeps in England, impressive curtain walls and a deep moat. It is in the care of English Heritage.

From Middleham, the walk takes us to the River Cover and along its banks. After crossing Hullo Bridge the path ascends to Braithwaite Hall. Owned by the National Trust and open by appointment only, this is a modest farmhouse of 1667, with three fine gables and unusual oval windows beneath them. Inside are stone floors, a fine oak staircase and panelling all from the late 17th century. On the hillside behind are the earthworks of a hill fort, thought to be Iron Age. After the hall, the lane eventually crosses Coverham Bridge, probably built by the monks of nearby Coverham Abbey. There are a few remains of the abbey, founded in the 12th century, mostly incorporated into later buildings. Miles Coverdale, the first man to complete a full English translation of the Bible, came from here.

Middleham – the Lambourn of the North

For many people, Middleham is the home of famous racehorses, and you may be lucky enough to see some in training as you walk over Middleham Low Moor towards the end of the walk – make sure you keep out of their way. More than 500 horses train in Middleham, under the watchful eyes of 13 trainers. Both the Low Moor and the High Moor have been used for exercise for more than 300 years; one of the earliest recorded winners was Bay

Bolton, born in 1705, which won Queen Anne's Gold Cup at York Races. Among early jockeys was the splendidly-named 'Crying Jackie' Mangle, who won the St Leger five times in the 1770s and 80s.

To your left as you leave the Low Moor and make your way back to the castle is William's Hill, the remains of the original motte-and-bailey castle built here by the Normans after 1066 to guard the approaches to Wensleydale and Coverdale. The motte, 40ft (12m) high, is joined by a curved bailey surrounded by a ditch. It was abandoned about 1170 when the new castle was begun near by.

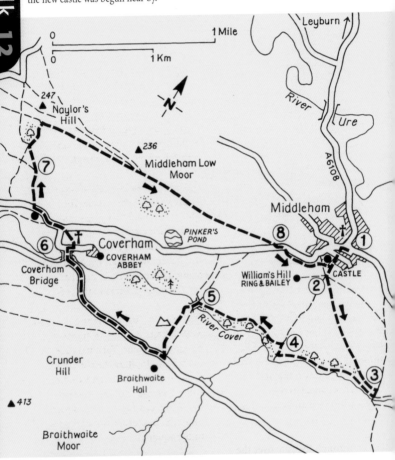

Walk 12 Directions

① From the cross in the **Square**, walk uphill past the **Black Swan Hotel**. A few paces beyond, turn left up a narrow passage beside the **Castle Tea Rooms**, continuing across the road and left of the **castle** to a gate.

② Go half left across the field, following the sign pointing towards the stepping stones. Cross the next three fields, over the waymarked stiles. After the third field, turn along the side of the field, ignoring a track to the right. Turn right at a waymarked crossing wall down to the bank of the **River Cover** by the stepping stones.

③ Turn right (do not cross the stepping stones) and follow the riverside path, going through a gate and up some steps. After returning to the riverbank, go right where the path forks. Go over two more stiles, turning immediately right after the second. Follow the waymark uphill to a marker post.

WHAT TO LOOK FOR ℹ

If you are very lucky you may see the iridescent blue and orange of the **kingfisher**, fishing above the waters of the River Cover. Vulnerable both to pollution and the ravages of a harsh winter, the kingfisher lives in the banks of the river, digging out a burrow up to 3ft (1m) deep. At the end a nest is constructed for the female to lay six or seven eggs. Young kingfishers are fed mainly with small fish – minnow and sticklebacks. Kingfishers catch fish with their fearsome bills and carry them back to their perches overlooking the stream. They carefully turn them so the head faces outwards from the bill, and hit them against the perch to stun or kill them, before swallowing them whole.

④ Turn left and follow the line of the wood. At the end of the field go left through a waymarked stile, through the trees to a second stile, then straight down the field back to the riverbank. Go over a waymarked stile and onward to the bridge.

⑤ Go through the gate over the bridge. Follow the track as it winds right and uphill through two gates on to a road, opposite **Braithwaite Hall**. Turn right, and follow the road for a mile (1.6km) to **Coverham Bridge**. Turn right over the bridge, then right again.

⑥ Before the gates, turn left through a small gate, walk beside a waterfall and into the churchyard.

WHERE TO EAT AND DRINK ℹ

Several of Middleham's hotels and inns offer meals and snacks as well as drinks. The **White Swan** has bar meals and a noted restaurant, open lunchtime and evenings. **Millers House Hotel** has dinners (weekends only in winter). The **Stable Door Restaurant** is open most lunchtimes and evenings and offers good home-cooked food.

Leave by the lychgate and turn left along the road. After ¼ mile (400m) go through a gate on the right opposite a disused factory, bearing slightly left. Go over three stiles. Go through a gate, pass between buildings and go over three stiles through a belt of woodland.

⑦ Cross the field to a gateway right of the wood. After passing the house, bend left to a gate on to a track. Turn right, go through a gate and turn right again. Don't follow the track, but go half left to meet a bridleway across the moor. Follow it for 1½ miles (2.4km) to the road.

⑧ Turn left. Just before the **Middleham** sign, take a signposted path on the right. Turn left over the stile and follow the path parallel to the road. Go through two more stiles, then take another towards the castle, passing through a gate on to the lane. Turn left and return to the square.

WHILE YOU'RE THERE ℹ

Nearby **Wensley**, after which the dale takes its name, was once a market town, but an outbreak of the plague in 1563 reduced it to this little village. Visit the church to see the monumental brass to the priest Simon de Wensley – one of the best in the country – and the wonderful out-of-place Scrope family pew, partly made of the rood screen from Easby Abbey near Richmond.

Whittington Without a Cat

A walk from Kirkby Lonsdale, returning along the banks of the River Lune.

•DISTANCE•	4¾ miles (7.7km)
•MINIMUM TIME•	2hrs 30min
•ASCENT / GRADIENT•	197ft (60m)
•LEVEL OF DIFFICULTY•	
•PATHS•	A little overgrown and indistinct in patches, quiet lanes and tracks, plenty of stiles
•LANDSCAPE•	Rolling hills, farmland, riverbank, good distance views
•SUGGESTED MAP•	aqua3 OS Explorer OL2 Yorkshire Dales – Southern & Western
•START / FINISH•	Grid reference: SD 615782
•DOG FRIENDLINESS•	On lead through farmland
•PARKING•	Devil's Bridge car park, Kirkby Lonsdale (free of charge)
•PUBLIC TOILETS•	None on route
•CONTRIBUTOR•	Sheila Bowker

BACKGROUND TO THE WALK

It's something of a revelation, to escape the weekend motorcycle congregation on Devil's Bridge and take this circular walk over rolling hills, through farmland and woods, to the worthy village of Whittington then to return along the banks of the lovely Lune. You pass close to Sellet Mill, its huge waterwheel, incorporated within the building, was reputedly once the second largest in the country. Corn was ground at the mill until its closure in the 1940s. Sellet is a word you'll come across often on this walk and is apparently an old local word for drumlin (a small rounded hill formed by glacial deposits). Your next Sellet is Sellet Bank, which appears to be a large drumlin. The walk takes you around its base and eventually to Sellet Hall. Built as a farm in 1570 by the Baines family, the hall was possibly used at sometime as a hospital, as it is situated at the end of Hosticle Lane – hosticle is an old dialect word for hospital. You return to Kirkby Lonsdale along the banks of the River Lune, following part of the Lune Valley Ramble.

The Devil's Bridge

A simple spring in a field at Newbiggin-on-Lune is the source of the beautiful River Lune, which eventually flows into Morecambe Bay and the Irish Sea to the north of Cockersand Abbey. The river has inspired many artists, most famously J M W Turner, who visited Kirkby Lonsdale in 1818 and subsequently included the river in two of his paintings .The riverbed is rocky under Devil's Bridge, so called because it was supposedly provided by the Devil to enable a poor widow to reach her cow on the other side of the river. In return for this the Devil was to acquire the soul of the first being to cross the bridge. The widow's only other possession was a small dog. According to a popular poem from the 1820s, she threw a bun across the bridge and the poor hound scampered after it, thus thwarting the Devil and saving her own soul. This graceful, three arched monument probably dates from the 14th century and no longer has to support the busy A65, which has had its own river crossing a short way downstream since the 1930s.

Walk 13 Directions

① From the west bank of the river, a few paces downstream from **Devil's Bridge**, take the path signposted 'Whittington' across a park with picnic tables to the **A65**. Cross over, go through a narrow meadow and between houses and almost immediately cross the **B6254**. As you enter another meadow, go uphill, keeping the walled wooded area on your left. Yellow markers and a sign to Wood End help you find the route. Keep on over the brow of the hill and straight ahead through two stiles. Turn left at another gap stile into the farmyard at **Wood End Farm**.

② Turn right on the farm track towards white painted **Wood End Cottage**. Go left in front of the cottage along an overgrown, walled path down to **Sellet Mill**. A stream comes in from the left and tries to take over the path, but drier ground is just around the corner. The path opens out by the mill race with good views of Ingleborough over the water.

③ Turn right by the cluster of homesteads and walk up the field, keeping the fence to your left, until level with the end of a garden. Go left through a yellow marked gate and walk straight across a small field to another marked gate followed immediately by a shallow stream. Bear right to go round **Sellet Bank**, aiming initially for the corner of a hedge under a row of pylons. Continue with the hedge to your right, taking time to look back at good views of Leck Fell and Barbon Fell.

WHAT TO LOOK FOR ⓘ

Leck Fell at 2,058ft (627m) is the highest point in present day Lancashire (although Coniston Old Man is the highest point in the 'old' Lancashire). The fell is worth visiting for its limestone scenery and archaeological sites, while below ground is a popular network of caving systems.

---

④ Go through a yellow marked stile on your right, then bear left round a wooded area. Facing **Sellet Hall**, turn right adjacent to the fenced driveway following the marker arrows, then keep on over the corner of the field to cross a stile and drop down a couple of steps to the road at a T-junction. Turn left along **Hosticle Lane** towards Whittington village.

⑤ The tall trees of **Hagg Wood** are away on your right and beech and hawthorn hedges are beside you as you follow the lane down to Whittington.

WHERE TO EAT AND DRINK ⓘ

There are usually a couple of vans at Devil's Bridge, one selling ices and the other drinks and snacks. The **Dragon's Head** pub in Whittington opens from 12 noon to 3PM every lunchtime except Monday and serves a selection of hot and cold food.

---

⑥ Go left at the T-junction for a few paces then cross the road and turn right over a pebbled mosaic at the entrance to the **Church of St Michael the Archangel**. Keep the square bell tower on your left before descending stone steps to go through a narrow stile and the modern graveyard. Proceed through a gate in the left corner and cross straight over two small fields to a stone stile leading to a narrow, walled lane that leads on to **Main Street**. Turn right, in front of a lovely building dated 1875, and on through the village past the village hall and the **Dragon's Head** pub.

⑦ At a sharp right bend on the edge of the village turn left along a sandy track, passing a farm and tennis courts. Follow the lane as it bends its way between fields to reach a pair of gates. Go through the gates on the left. Bear left to pick up the riverside walk – the **Lune Valley Ramble** – back to the **A65** bridge at **Kirkby Lonsdale**. Go through a gate and up steps to the left of the parapet. Cross the road, drop down the other side to cross the park at the start of the walk.

WHILE YOU'RE THERE ⓘ

Visit **Kirkby Lonsdale** which has a market charter from the 13th century, and still holds a weekly market, around the unusual 20th-century butter cross, every Thursday. There are some fine 17th- and 18th-century buildings and the famous views from the churchyard.

Around Ribblehead's Majestic Viaduct

Beside and beneath a great monument to Victorian engineering.

•DISTANCE•	5 miles (8km)
•MINIMUM TIME•	2hrs
•ASCENT / GRADIENT•	328ft (100m) ▲ ▲ ▲
•LEVEL OF DIFFICULTY•	🚶🚶 🚶 🚶
•PATHS•	Moorland and farm paths and tracks, 2 stiles
•LANDSCAPE•	Bleak moorland and farmland, dominated by the Ribblehead viaduct
•SUGGESTED MAP•	aqua3 OS Explorer OL2 Yorkshire Dales – Southern & Western
•START / FINISH•	Grid reference: SD 765792
•DOG FRIENDLINESS•	Off lead by viaduct, but should be on leads in farmland
•PARKING•	Parking space at junction of B6255 and B6479 near Ribblehead viaduct
•PUBLIC TOILETS•	None on route
•CONTRIBUTOR•	David Winpenny

BACKGROUND TO THE WALK

'Nowhere in the kingdom has nature placed such gigantic obstacles in the way of the railway engineer', observed a newspaper when the Settle-to-Carlisle railway line was complete. The railway was planned and built by the Midland Railway so it could reach Scotland without trespassing on its rivals' territory of the east or west coast routes. It cost the then enormous sum of £3,500,000 and was opened in 1876. Its construction included building 20 big viaducts and 14 tunnels. At the height of the works, 6,000 men were employed, living in shanty towns beside the line and giving the area a flavour of the Wild West. The line survived for almost 100 years, until passenger services were withdrawn in 1970. It was said that the viaducts, especially the Ribblehead, were unsafe. There was a public outcry which led to a concerted campaign to keep the line open. Since then there has been a change of heart. Ribblehead is repaired, and the line is one of the most popular – and spectacular – tourist lines in the country.

Ribblehead – 'A Mighty Work'

It took five years to build Ribblehead's huge viaduct. It's ¼ mile (400m) long, and is 100ft (30m) high at its maximum; the columns stretch another 25ft (7.6m) into the ground. The stone – more than 30,000 cubic yards (22,950 cubic m) of it – came from Littledale to the north, and construction progressed from north to south. The area is called Batty Moss, and was inhospitable, to say the least. There is a rumour that the columns are set on bales of wool, as the engineers could not find the bedrock. Romantic as this might sound in a county whose fortunes are largely based on wool, it's untrue. They are set in concrete on top of rock. There are 24 spans, each 45ft (13.7m) wide. Every sixth column is thicker than its neighbours so that if one fell it would take only five others with it, not the whole viaduct.

Blea Moor and Ancient Farms

The walk takes you past the viaduct to the beginning of Blea Moor, and near perhaps the most exposed signal box in Britain. Beyond it is Blea Moor tunnel, another of the mighty engineering works of the Settle-to-Carlisle Railway, 2,629yds (2,400m) long and dug by miners working by candlelight. They got through £50-worth of candles each month. The advent of the miners and the huge paraphernalia of Victorian engineering must have seemed astonishing to the farmers sheltering at the foot of Whernside. With their ancient, Norse-inspired names – Winterscales, Broadrake, Gunnerfleet – their farms are an enduring testimony to the resilience of man long before he tried to tame it with such forces.

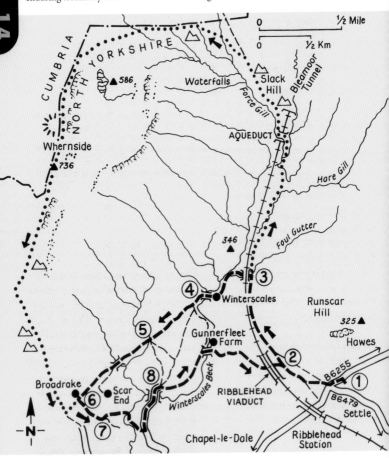

Walk 14 Directions

① From the parking place, cross the road and take the boardwalk by the sign towards the viaduct to a track. Turn right and follow the track until it turns under the viaduct; continue straight ahead.

② Continue walking, now parallel with the railway line above you to your left. Go past a **Three Peaks** signboard, following the **Whernside** sign. Go over a gated wooden stile and continue until you reach a railway signal. Go left under the railway arch, following the public bridleway sign.

③ Go through a gate at the end of the arch and follow the track downhill towards the stream, then bear left towards farm buildings. Go through a gate between the buildings and on to a humpback bridge by a cottage.

④ Follow the lane over two cattle grids, through a wooden gate by a barn, then through a metal gate, to wind through the farm buildings. Go through another metal gate then a waymarked wooden gate.

WHERE TO EAT AND DRINK ⓘ

In the summer months an **ice cream van** stations itself at the Ribblehead viaduct car park, and **Winterscales Farm** sometimes offers teas. The **Station Inn**, near the viaduct, offers home-cooked meals in its bar and dining room.

---

⑤ Walk along a track through the fields, going over a small bridge of railway sleepers. By a sign to **Scar End**, bear right to a small gate. Go across three fields, through a series of gates and continue ahead through the next field, to reach farm buildings.

⑥ Turn left by the farm down the farm track. Where it bends right, go over the cattle grid and turn sharp left round the fence and on to a track, following the bridleway sign, to a ladder stile.

⑦ The obvious track winds through fields to reach a stream bed (dry in summer). Cross this,

---

WHILE YOU'RE THERE ⓘ

Take the road – or the train – up to Dent Station. You will pass through the Blea Moor tunnel and then over the Dent Head viaduct, with its ten spans, and the same maximum height as Ribblehead. If you want to visit Dent itself, once in Yorkshire and now adrift in Cumbria, it's a long walk; the station is more than 4 miles (6.4km) from the village!

---

and continue along the track to meet a road near a cattle grid. Turn left and walk down the road and over a bridge.

⑧ Where the road divides, go right, through a gate, towards the viaduct. At the next gate go right again over a footbridge by the farm buildings. Continue through two more gates and follow the track under the viaduct, continuing towards the road and the parking place.

Extending the Walk

You can extend this walk to take in one of the famous Three Peaks, **Whernside**. Leave the main route at Point ③, following the signpost for Dent. After about a mile (1.6km), cross the railway line and ascend steeply by **Force Gill**. Follow the sign to **Whernside** and a path, paved in parts to prevent erosion, alongside a wall. From the summit you can descend to the south on a steep path which will bring you to meet up with the main walk near the buildings of **Broadrake**. This is Point ⑥ and you turn right to return to **Ribblehead**.

WHAT TO LOOK FOR ⓘ

On a fine summer's day Ribblehead can seem a magical place, with the curlews calling, the sheep bleating and the occasional rumble as a train crosses the viaduct. But it can also be one of the bleakest places in the Dales. The average rainfall in the area is 70in (177.8cm), but can often be half as much again. Snow frequently blocks the roads. Wind speeds of 50 knots are a normal occurrence and gales can reach even greater speeds. Crossing the viaduct then becomes a hazardous business.

Dalesfolk Traditions in Hubberholme

From J B Priestley's favourite Dales village, along Langstrothdale and back.

•DISTANCE•	5 miles (8km)
•MINIMUM TIME•	2hrs
•ASCENT / GRADIENT•	394ft (120m) ▲▲▲
•LEVEL OF DIFFICULTY•	👫 👫 👫
•PATHS•	Field paths and tracks, steep after Yockenthwaite, 11 stiles
•LANDSCAPE•	Streamside paths and limestone terrace
•SUGGESTED MAP•	aqua3 OS Explorer OL30 Yorkshire Dales – Northern & Central
•START / FINISH•	Grid reference: SD 927782
•DOG FRIENDLINESS•	Dogs should be on lead, except on section between Yockenthwaite and Cray
•PARKING•	Beside river in village, opposite church (not church parking)
•PUBLIC TOILETS•	None on route
•CONTRIBUTOR•	David Winpenny

BACKGROUND TO THE WALK

Literary pilgrims visit Hubberholme to see the George Inn, where J B Priestley could often be found enjoying the local ale, and the churchyard, the last resting place for his ashes, as he requested. He chose an idyllic spot. Set at the foot of Langstrothdale, Hubberholme is a cluster of old farmhouses and cottages surrounding the church. Norman in origin, St Michael's was once flooded so badly that fish were seen swimming in the nave. One vicar of Hubberholme is said to have carelessly baptised a child Amorous instead of Ambrose, a mistake that, once entered in the parish register, couldn't be altered. Amorous Stanley used his memorable name later in life as part of his stock-in-trade as a hawker.

Church Wood

Hubberholme church's best treasures are of wood. The rood loft above the screen is one of only two surviving in Yorkshire, (the other is at Flamborough, far away on the east coast). Once holding figures of Christ on the Cross, St Mary and St John, it dates from 1558, when such examples of Popery were fast going out of fashion. It still retains some of its once-garish colouring of red, gold and black. Master-carver Robert Thompson provided almost all the rest of the furniture in 1934 – look for his mouse trademark on each piece.

Ancient Yockenthwaite and Remote Cray

Yockenthwaite's name, said to have been derived from an ancient Irish name, Eogan, conjures up images of the ancient past. Norse settlers were here more than 1,000 years ago – and even earlier settlers have left their mark, a Bronze-Age stone circle a little further up the valley. The hamlet now consists of a few farm buildings beside the bridge over the Wharfe at the end of Langstrothdale Chase, a Norman hunting ground which used to have its own forest laws and punishments. You walk along a typical Dales limestone terrace to reach Cray, on the road over from Bishopdale joining Wharfedale to Wensleydale. Here is another huddle of farmhouses, around the White Lion Inn. You then follow the Cray Gill downstream, past a series of small cascades. For a more spectacular waterfall, head up the road from the inn a little way to Cray High Bridge.

Burning the Candle

Back in Hubberholme, the George Inn was once the vicarage. It is the scene each New Year's Day of an ancient auction. It begins with the lighting of a candle, after which the auctioneer asks for bids for the year's tenancy of the 'Poor Pasture', a 16-acre (7.2ha) field behind the inn. All bids have to be completed before the candle burns out. In the days when the George housed the vicar, he ran the auction. Today a local auctioneer takes the role, and a merry time is had by all. The proceeds from the auction go to help the old people of the village.

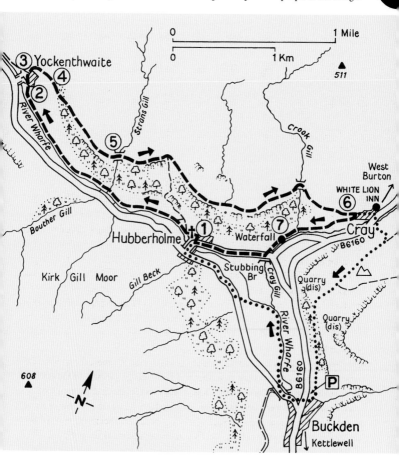

Walk 15 Directions

① Go through a **Dales Way** signed gate near the east end of the church, bend left and then take the lower

path, signed '**Yockenthwaite**'. Walk beside the river for 1¼ miles (2km) through three stiles, a gate and two more stiles. The path eventually rises to another stone stile into **Yockenthwaite**.

Walk 15

WHERE TO EAT AND DRINK ⓘ

The **George Inn** in Hubberholme has an enviable reputation for its food and its real ale, as well as its convivial atmosphere. The same is true of the **White Lion** at Cray – slightly off the route. Both are typical Dales inns, and worth a detour.

② Go through the stile and bend left to a wooden gate. Continue through a farm gate by a sign to **Deepdale and Beckermonds**. Before the track reaches a bridge go right and swing round to a sign to **Cray and Hubberholme**.

③ Go up the hill and, as the track curves right, continue to follow the **Cray and Hubberholme** sign. Part-way up the hill go right at a footpath sign through a wooden gate in a fence.

④ Go through a second gate to a footpath sign and ascend the hillside. Go through a gap in a wall by another signpost and follow the obvious path through several gaps in crossing walls. Go over two stone stiles and ascend again to a footbridge between stiles.

⑤ Cross the bridge and continue through woodland to another stile. Wind round the head of the valley and follow the signpost to **Cray**. Go over a footbridge. The footpath winds its way down the valley side. Go through a gate and straight ahead across meadow land to a

gateway on to a track, and on to a stone barn.

⑥ Bend to the right beyond the barn, down to a public footpath sign to **Stubbing Bridge**. Go down the path between stone walls and through a wooden gate and on to the grassy hillside. Pass another footpath sign and continue downhill to meet the stream by a waterfall.

⑦ Continue along the streamside path through woodland. Go over a wooden stile and on past a barn to a stone stile on to the road. Turn right along the road back to the parking place in **Hubberholme**.

Extending the Walk

This walk can be extended by continuing, from Point ⑥, to the White Lion at Cray. Cross the valley to join a path into Buckden. Take the riverside path, which brings you back to the road to Hubberholme.

WHILE YOU'RE THERE ⓘ

If you've the energy, a walk to the summit of nearby **Buckden Pike** will reward you with fine views and a memorial to five Polish airmen whose plane crashed there in November 1942. One man survived the crash, following a fox's footprints through the snow down to safety at a farm. The cross he erected has a fox's head set in the base as thanksgiving. Buckden Pike is best climbed up the track called Walden Road from Starbotton.

WHAT TO LOOK FOR ⓘ

A number of barns in the area have been converted to become holiday accommodation **bunk barns**. An initiative set up by the Yorkshire Dales National Park Authority and the Countryside Commission in 1979, the aim is to solve two problems – how to preserve the now-redundant barns that are so vital a part of the Dales landscape, and a lack of simple accommodation for walkers. These bunkhouse barns offer farmers an alternative to letting the barns decay. They add basic amenities for cooking, washing and sleeping (and sometimes extras like comfortable chairs!) and let them to families or groups.

Horsehouse and Coverdale

A moorside and riverside walk in one of the loveliest valleys in the Dales.

•DISTANCE•	6½ miles (10.4km)
•MINIMUM TIME•	2hrs 30min
•ASCENT / GRADIENT•	459ft (140m) ▲ ▲ ▲
•LEVEL OF DIFFICULTY•	🚶 🚶 🚶
•PATHS•	Field, moorland and riverside paths and tracks, 31 stiles
•LANDSCAPE•	Farmed valley and moorland, with River Cover
•SUGGESTED MAP•	aqua3 OS Explorer OL30 Yorkshire Dales – Northern & Central
•START / FINISH•	Grid reference: SE 047813
•DOG FRIENDLINESS•	Sheep in fields, so keep dogs on lead
•PARKING•	Roadside parking below former school in Horsehouse
•PUBLIC TOILETS•	None on route
•CONTRIBUTOR•	David Winpenny

BACKGROUND TO THE WALK

It seems hard to believe that the quiet village of Horsehouse was once a place bustling with traffic, as stagecoaches and packhorse trains passed through it on one of the main coaching routes from London to the North. The two inns that existed in the village served the travellers on their way to and from Richmond, one of the region's principal coaching centres. Beyond Horsehouse, to the south west, Coverdale grows steeper and wilder before the vertiginous descent down Park Rash into Kettlewell in Wharfedale – a journey that must have deeply scared many 17th- and 18th-century travellers. Trains of up to 40 packhorses also used the route, bringing goods to the valley and taking lead and other minerals from the mines on the moors above. Bells jingling on the harness of the leading horse signalled their presence.

Headless Pedlars and a Future King

Pedlars, too, followed the routes, and some at least seem to have met a gruesome end; three headless corpses were found by a side road into Nidderdale. The local constable initiated enquiries and the evidence suggested that they were Scottish pedlars, killed for their money and goods. Their heads were not found – nor were their murderers, though the local finger of suspicion pointed strongly at a Horsehouse innkeeper and her daughter.

West Scrafton, a tiny village set beside Great Gill as it tumbles towards the River Cover below, is dominated by the heights of Great Roova Crags (1549ft/472m). Before the dissolution of the monasteries in the 1530s, the village was owned by the monks of Jervaulx Abbey. Much of the land was subsequently in the hands of the Earl of Lennox – and West Scrafton Manor House is said to have been the birthplace of his son Lord Darnley, murdered second husband of Mary, Queen of Scots and father of King James I and VI. Carlton-in-Coverdale, the next village on the walk is the largest of all the dale's settlements, with some good houses lining the main street and the motte of a small castle visible south of the main street. Flatts Farm at the west end of the village has an inscription to Henry Constantine 'The Coverdale Poet'.

Miles Coverdale, the first man to translate the whole Bible into English, was born in the valley – no one knows exactly where – in 1488. After some time as a friar in Cambridge, his reforming zeal meant he was forced to live abroad. The first edition of his bible was published in Paris in 1535, and a revised version, known as the Great Bible, in 1538. From 1551 he was Bishop of Exeter, but he was imprisoned under Mary Tudor. In Elizabeth's reign he lived and preached in London until his death in 1568.

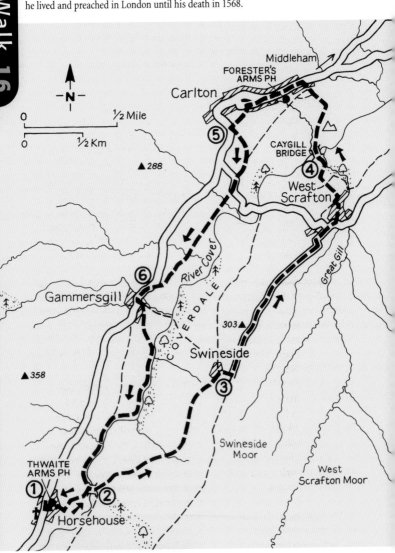

Walk 16 Directions

① Walk past the **Thwaite Arms**, then curve behind it on a track. Turn right down a signed track, go through two gates, then bend left to a third gate. Beyond it bear half right to a gate and footbridge.

② Cross the bridge and bear left. Go over a stile signed 'Swineside', cross a small field to another stile then bear half right. Cross a track and follow a wall to a stile. Bear left, eventually on a track, through two stiles, then go half left to a signed stile. Climb the grassy path to a gap in the wall, then take the lower path towards buildings. Go through a stile and a gateway, then bend right to a gate, to the right of the buildings.

③ After the gate, follow the track past the farmhouse then right, uphill. At the top, go over a cattle grid and follow the metalled lane for 1½ miles (2.4km) into **West Scrafton**. In the village take a track to the left signed 'No Through Road'. Turn left signed 'Carlton', then turn right. After a gate and a walled section, turn left down the field. Go through a kissing gate and right of a barn, towards **Caygill Bridge**. Bear right, following the wooded valley, though a gate and down to two footbridges.

④ After the bridges, go through a gate and ascend steeply, past a signpost. At the top bear right

alongside a wall and on to a gate. Follow the footpath sign left, eventually reaching **Carlton**. Turn left along the road passing the **Forester's Arms**. Where it widens, bear left between cottages following a footpath sign to a stile. Continue through six more stiles to a road.

⑤ Turn left and go immediately though a gate. Descend to a stile, bear right above a barn to another stile and follow a wall to a stile on to a road. Turn left. At a left bend, go right, over a stile signed 'Gammersgill'. Go over two more stiles and cross a stream to a waymarked gate. Cross the fields, going over a stile and a wooden footbridge, and through a gate. Where the walled lane bends right, go ahead through a stile, then bear right to a stile on to the road.

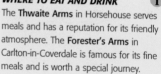

⑥ Turn left into **Gammersgill**, cross the bridge, then turn left though a gate signed 'Swineside'. Bear right to another gate, then cross to a stile beside a gate. Bear half left to the field corner and go over a stile. Now follow the river over five more stiles and past a stone bridge. After another stile reach the footbridge crossed near the start of the walk. Retrace your steps back to **Horsehouse**.

Walk 17

Mr Danby's Druidic Dream

A gentle walk from a peculiar mock-druidic temple though rich farmland near Masham.

•DISTANCE•	4¼ miles (6.8km)
•MINIMUM TIME•	2hrs
•ASCENT / GRADIENT•	426ft (130m) ▲ ▲ ▲
•LEVEL OF DIFFICULTY•	👫 👫 👫
•PATHS•	Tracks and field paths, 7 stiles
•LANDSCAPE•	Valley and farmland, with some surprising constructions
•SUGGESTED MAP•	aqua3 OS Explorer 298 Nidderdale
•START / FINISH•	Grid reference: SE 177787
•DOG FRIENDLINESS•	Keep dogs on leads or under close control
•PARKING•	Car park by Druid's Temple
•PUBLIC TOILETS•	None on route
•CONTRIBUTOR•	David Winpenny

BACKGROUND TO THE WALK

Start or finish the walk with a druidical flourish by visiting the Druid's Temple – one of the most extraordinary of Yorkshire's rich crop of follies. It was created on the orders of William Danby, eccentric master of nearby Swinton Castle, in 1809. One of his purposes was philanthropy – there was widespread unemployment in Nidderdale, and he saw his version of Stonehenge as an early job creation scheme. What his workers thought when they were paid to build something so strange is not recorded; they were no doubt supposed to remain silent – and grateful.

The Hermit and the Luminous Moss

Danby's Druid's Temple bears only superficial resemblance to Stonehenge. It is oval, not round, and sits in a hollow, solidly lined with great upright stones. At the opposite end from the entrance is a cave, said to contain a rare type of luminous moss. And outside the Temple, like tugs around an ocean liner, are pretend cromlechs, consisting of huge flat stones on uprights. These betray the early 19th-century origins of the temple – they are spaced with perfect symmetry, in the best classical tradition. Less classical, though very fashionable, was the hermit who is said to have inhabited the cave for four and a half years, without cutting his hair or beard.

    The walk passes through what was perhaps a trial run for the splendours of the Druid's Temple, a gateway of massively piled boulders, before descending towards the valley of the Pott Beck – a reminder that the area, for council purposes, goes under the delightful name of Ilton-cum-Pott. You will see the dam wall of Leighton Reservoir ahead (you can see the reservoir itself from just beyond the Druid's Temple). It was under construction at the outbreak of the First World War (the neighbouring Roundhill Reservoir had been constructed more than ten years before), and the engineering works were served by a light railway from Masham. As war broke out, the site was taken over by the 1st Leeds Battalion – the Leeds Pals – who were stationed here for nine months, before being transferred first to Ripon, then, via Hampshire and Egypt, to the Somme.

Spurring On

Much of the walk follows the Ripon Rowel Walk, a 50-mile (80km) circular route centred on the city of Ripon, and officially starting from the cathedral. It is, appropriately, named after the rowels – the small spiked wheels fitted to the back of a horserider's spurs – that were Ripon's speciality in the 16th and 17th centuries. So renowned were the rowels manufactured here that a royal charter recognised their superiority, and they gave rise to a common folk saying 'As true steel as Ripon rowels'. A spur appears in the city's coat of arms (along with a horn) and can be seen on the top of the 300-year-old obelisk in the Market Square. Many local clubs and societies also use this symbol in their emblems and even their titles. The Ripon Rowel Walk is well waymarked by a spiked wheel symbol.

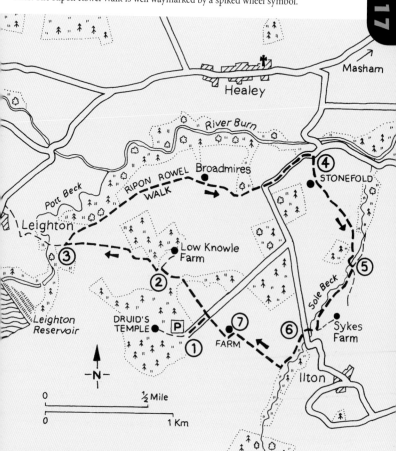

Walk 17 Directions

① Park in the car park by the **Druid's Temple** (to visit the Temple, walk though the wood, then return to the car park) and walk down the road you drove up.

Just after a row of metal posts, cross a stile on the left marked with the Ripon Rowel Walk symbol, opposite a farm track. Walk ahead across the field and go though a gate surrounded by boulders. Bend left, along the edge of the wood and at the farm track go left to a gate.

Walk 17

② After the gate turn right following the track. It bends away from the wood and down to a ladder stile. After the stile, bear half left across the field towards the pine trees to a stile in a crossing wire fence. Continue ahead, over the ridge of the hill, to descend by a small wood to two waymarked wooden posts.

③ At the posts turn sharp right, uphill, on the grassy track. Follow the track through five gates. Near a farmhouse go through another gate and walk to the right of the buildings. After a gateway the track becomes a metalled lane. At a road junction continue straight ahead. As the road begins to descend, turn right through a metal gate towards **Stonefold** farm.

WHERE TO EAT AND DRINK ⓘ

There is nowhere in the immediate vicinity, but a visit to Masham will offer a good choice of both pubs and cafés. The **Bistro** in the Black Sheep Brewery is recommended. For a village pub, try the **Crown Inn** at Grewelthorpe, which serves good meals.

---

④ Walk through the farmyard, past the buildings, then bear left through a gateway into a field. Go through a gate on the right and then half left towards a row of trees to another gate. After the gate, go half right across the field through a gateway in a crossing fence and descend into a valley. Turn right, beside the stream, then half right through a metal gate and over a stile in a wire fence to a footbridge.

⑤ Cross the bridge and go over a waymarked stile, then turn right, along a track. Go through two gates, past a barn, and through another metal gate on to a lane.

WHILE YOU'RE THERE ⓘ

Island Heritage at Pott Hall Farm by Leighton Reservoir has a wide range of primitive, domesticated sheep from around Britain, including Hebridean, Manx Loghtan, North Ronaldsway and Shetland. According to the season you can see young lambs, watch the shearing or see the fleeces being sorted for spinning. A shop sells many unusual woollen products.

---

⑥ Turn left, then turn right up the next track. Go over a stile beside a gate, and along the track. After a gateway, turn right alongside a wall toward the farm on the ridge. Climb the hill on the track and go through a metal gate, then over a stile in a wire fence.

⑦ After the stile bend to the left, following the fence, in front of the **farm building** then through a metal gate on your right-hand side. Follow the farm track, going through a metal gate, and continue to meet the metalled lane. Turn left back to the car park.

WHAT TO LOOK FOR ⓘ

As you approach Broadmires Farm, look across the valley to the village of **Healey**. A typical Nidderdale village of stone houses strung along a single main street, Healey has an extraordinary church. St Paul's was designed in 1848 by Edward Buckton Lamb, one of the so-called 'Rogue Architects' of the early Victorian period. He rejected the current ideas of historical precedent and worked entirely for picturesque effect. For a village church, St Paul's has big ideas, with a central tower and transepts, as well as a spire. Inside it has the most amazing timberwork, like the inside of a mad ship — a wooden, ecclesiastical equivalent of William Danby's Temple.

Herriot's Darrowby

James Herriot based his fictional home town on his real one – Thirsk.

•DISTANCE•	5 miles (8km)
•MINIMUM TIME•	2hrs
•ASCENT / GRADIENT•	66ft (20m)
•LEVEL OF DIFFICULTY•	
•PATHS•	Town paths, field paths and tracks, 6 stiles
•LANDSCAPE•	Streamside and undulating pastureland around town
•SUGGESTED MAP•	aqua3 OS Explorer 302 Northallerton & Thirsk
•START / FINISH•	Grid reference: SE 430813
•DOG FRIENDLINESS•	Keep dogs on lead
•PARKING•	Roadside parking in main street of Sowerby village
•PUBLIC TOILETS•	Thirsk town centre
•CONTRIBUTOR•	David Winpenny

BACKGROUND TO THE WALK

The elegant Georgian village street of Sowerby – now joined on to the town of Thirsk – is lined with a handsome avenue of lime trees. Such a civilised aspect belies the origins of the village's name, for Sowerby means the 'township in the muddy place'. Once you begin the walk, the reason becomes evident, even in dry weather. Sowerby is on the edge of the flood plain of the Cod Beck. Sowerby Flatts, which you will see across the beck at the start of the walk, and cross at the finish, is a popular venue for impromptu games of soccer and other sports, but is still prone to flooding.

Between Old and New

Once you've crossed the road by the end of New Bridge, you are walking between Old Thirsk and New Thirsk – though new in this context still means medieval. Old Thirsk is set to the east of the Cod Beck; like Sowerby, it too has a watery name, for Thirsk comes from an old Swedish word meaning a 'fen'. New Thirsk, to the west, is centred on the fine cobbled market place. The parish church, which you will pass twice, is the best Perpendicular church in North Yorkshire, with a particularly imposing tower.

South Kilvington, at the northern end of the walk, used to be a busy village on the main road north from Thirsk to Yarm. For much of the 19th century it was home to William Kingsley, who was vicar here until his death at the age of 101 in 1916 – having been born as Wellington defeated Napoleon at Waterloo. He entertained both the painter Turner and the art critic John Ruskin here – as well as his cousin Charles Kingsley, author of *The Water Babies*. More than a little eccentric, the vicar had signs in his garden saying 'Beware of Mantraps'. When asked where they were, he paraded his three housemaids.

Darrowby and Wight

For many visitors, the essential place to visit in Thirsk is Skeldale House in Kirkgate – on the right as you return from the church to the Market Square. This was the surgery of local vet James Wight, better known by his pen name, James Herriot. Now a museum, 'The World of James Herriot', this was where Wight worked for all his professional life. Thirsk itself is a major character in the books, appearing lightly disguised as Darrowby. The museum has reconstructions of what the surgery and the family rooms were like in the 1940s, and tells the history of veterinary science. Whether or not you're a fan of the Herriot tales, which began with *If Only They Could Talk* in 1970, you'll find it a fascinating and nostalgic tour.

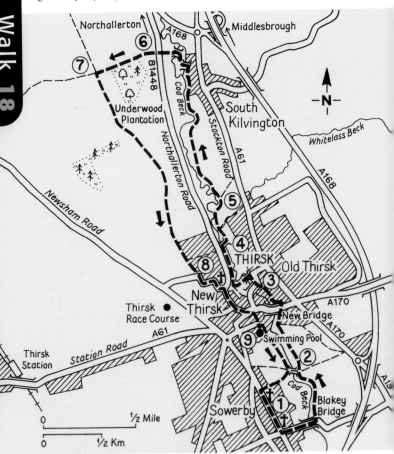

Walk 18 Directions

① Walk down the village street, away from **Thirsk**. Just past the Methodist Church on the left, go left down **Blakey Lane**. After the bridge turn left through a kissing gate and go through four kissing gates to reach a footbridge.

② Continue along the path, with the stream on your left, to a stile and go through two gates to a car park, keeping straight ahead to the road. Cross it and take a path that curves left then right by the bridge. At a paved area turn right, to go alongside a green to a road.

③ Cross and continue beside the houses, going left at the top of the green. Cross the metal bridge and continue beside the beck opposite the east end of the church. Before reaching the road take the path to the right, beside a bench, to a footbridge on the right.

Walk 18

④ Cross the bridge, go through two gates and curve left to follow the beck to a gate by a bridge. Go straight ahead (not over the bridge) and follow the path across the fields, veering slightly right to a stile on your right.

⑤ Go over the stile and follow the stream, going over another two stiles to pass beside houses. Continue left over a footbridge by some mill buildings. The path winds right to a second footbridge. Follow the bridleway sign across the field through two more gates to reach the main road.

⑥ Cross the road and go through a signed gate opposite, to another gate beside a wood. At an open space past the wood, turn left through a gap in the hedge, opposite a waymark to the right.

⑦ Walk down the field with a hedge on your left. In the second field go left over a stile and continue with the hedge on your right to another stile. Bear left to meet a path that crosses the field and becomes a grassy lane between hedges, then a track.

⑧ At a metalled road go straight ahead, bearing left then right past the church tower. Turn right and walk into the town centre. In the

WHERE TO EAT AND DRINK

Thirsk has a good choice of cafés, pubs and hotels. Recommended are the upmarket **Golden Fleece** and the **Three Tuns** in the Market Place. The **Lord Nelson** has bar meals and Sunday lunches, while **Yorks Tea Rooms**, also in the Market Place, offers good lunches and a range of coffees. In Sowerby, **Sheppard's Hotel and Restaurant** offers lunch and dinner.

Market Place head half left towards the Three Tuns Inn, and down a signed passageway by the drycleaners.

⑨ Cross the road diagonally right and go towards the swimming pool entrance. Turn left and bend round the pool building to a gate. Go ahead to a gate and alongside the beck. At the bridge turn right across the field on a grassy track to a gate on to a lane. Go straight ahead to return to **Sowerby** village street.

WHILE YOU'RE THERE

Visit the **Thirsk Museum and tourist information centre** at 14 Kirkgate. As well as having interesting local exhibits and displays, this was the birthplace, in November 1756, of Thomas Lord. The son of a local farmer, Thomas made his name as a professional cricketer, and set up his own ground in Dorset Square in 1787. Lord's Cricket Ground moved to its present site in 1814.

WHAT TO LOOK FOR

See if you can catch a film at the **Ritz Cinema**, just off the Market Place. Built in 1912, it went under several names during its 80-year history, finally closing in 1992 as Studio One. For the previous ten years it had been kept going by a dedicated husband and wife team, but the economics of local cinemas had become almost impossible. The people of Thirsk were determined to have films back in their town, however, and, under the control of Thirsk Town Council, it was reopened in March 1995, reverting to its original name and on a six-month lease. So successful was it, that it still continues to show a regular programme of films. It is now run entirely by volunteers. Its equipment – including a horn-shaped loudspeaker above the screen dating from the 1930s – has been updated, but the Ritz still retains the atmosphere of a typical small-town cinema of the past.

Walk 19

Ingleton and its Falls

A renowned walk by the falls, on a route first opened for tourists in 1885.

•DISTANCE•	5 miles (8km)
•MINIMUM TIME•	2hrs
•ASCENT / GRADIENT•	689ft (210m) ▲▲▲
•LEVEL OF DIFFICULTY•	👫👫👫
•PATHS•	Good paths and tracks, with some steps throughout
•LANDSCAPE•	Two wooded valleys, waterfalls, ancient track, wide views
•SUGGESTED MAP•	aqua3 OS Explorer OL2 Yorkshire Dales – Southern & Western
•START / FINISH•	Grid reference: SD 693733
•DOG FRIENDLINESS•	Dogs should be on leads by waterfalls
•PARKING•	Pay-and-display car park in centre of Ingleton, or at start of Waterfalls Walk
•PUBLIC TOILETS•	Ingleton
•NOTE•	Admission charge for Waterfalls Walk
•CONTRIBUTOR•	David Winpenny

BACKGROUND TO THE WALK

This is one of the classic walks of the Yorkshire Dales, and was first opened to visitors in 1885. A workaday town, and today one of the Dales' honeypots, Ingleton shows its mining and quarrying history in its buildings. It became a place for tourists to visit when the railway arrived in 1859 – the viaduct almost cuts the village in half. The entrepreneurs who developed the Waterfalls Walk in the 1880s, and charged for the privilege of taking the route, were tapping into the start of one of the most profitable of industries in the Dales.

Cascades and Strata
The spectacle of the Waterfalls Walk begins in Swilla Glen, where the River Twiss passes through a deep gorge, with rapids and whirlpools giving a taste of what is to come. The first of the cascades soon follows – Pecca Falls, where the river tumbles over a shelf of the hard greywacke stone, eating away at the softer slate beds below. Beyond, the narrow glen opens out as you approach Thornton Force. Unlike the other falls on the walk, this is not a series of rapids confined within the valley, but a majestic plunge of water 40ft (12m) from its lip of hard limestone into a pool gouged into the slate beds below, which have been heaved into a vertical position. This is one of the classic spots for studying the geology of the area; the different strata are conveniently exposed. A glacier came to this part of the valley – the tip of its nose reached just above the point where the water now falls. Here it deposited the mass of boulder clay it had pushed in front of it; the remains can still be made out beside the fall.

Limestone and Water
The route beyond follows Twisleton Lane, an ancient packhorse route on the line of the Roman road from Bainbridge to Ingleton. Above you are Twisleton Scars, great bands of limestone interspersed with horizontal bands of shale. One of the best limestone pavements in the area is to be found at the top of the Scars. The walk then joins the second of the

waterfall-filled valleys, this time of the River Doe, on its way back to Ingleton. The woodland here is some of the oldest and most unspoiled in the area, with ancient oak trees flanking the waterfalls. Eventually the route leaves the river and comes out into a former limestone quarry – there is still quarrying in the area, for the greywacke, which is used for road surfacing. Ingleton also once supported a number of cotton mills, powered by water diverted in mill races from the rivers.

Walk 19 Directions

① Leave the car park in the centre of **Ingleton** at its western end. Turn right along the road and follow the

'Waterfalls Walk' signs, which take you downhill and across the river to the entrance to the falls. Walk through the car park, pay the admission fee, and go through two kissing gates. The path goes

Walk 19

WHERE TO EAT AND DRINK ⓘ
As you would expect, Ingleton is well-served with places to eat and drink. There are refreshments available at the entrance to the **Waterfalls Walk** and beyond Pecca Falls. Among the recommended cafés are **Bernies**, **Fountain Café** and **Curlew Crafts and Tea Rooms**. **Inglenook Chippy** serves traditional fish and chips. The best of the pubs is the **Wheatsheaf**.

downwards then ascends steps. Cross **Manor Bridge** and continue upstream, now with the river on your left, to **Pecca Bridge**.

② Cross the bridge, and turn right, back on to the left bank of the stream. Continue to follow the path as it climbs uphill to reach **Thornton Force**. The path winds slightly away from the stream and up steps to pass the waterfall, and then takes you over **Ravenray Bridge**, and up more steps, to a kissing gate on to **Twisleton Lane**.

③ Turn right along the rough lane. Go through two gates, after which the track becomes metalled. Walk past the farm buildings, following 'Waterfalls Walk' signs. Go over a gated stone stile and along the track, then though a kissing gate and on to a road.

④ Go straight across the road, following the sign to Skirwith. Follow the path as it bends right, still following the 'Waterfall Walk' sign. Go through a gate, then another into woodland. The path passes **Beezley Falls** and **Rival Falls**. A little further down, take a path to the left on to a footbridge with a good view of the deep and narrow **Baxenghyll Gorge**. Continue to follow the path, which takes you to another footbridge.

WHILE YOU'RE THERE ⓘ
A visit to **White Scar Cave** will take you underground into one of the country's largest caverns, discovered in 1923. An 80-minute guided tour passes underground waterfalls and gives you the chance to study the massive stalagmites and stalactites, some with names such as Devil's Tongue, Judge's Head and Arum Lily. The entrance is on the B6255, just north of Ingleton.

⑤ Cross the bridge, go through a kissing gate, and then follow the path as it bends, at one point almost at water level, then going away from the water into trees. The path eventually brings you though former quarry workings. Continue through a hand gate on to a lane.

⑥ Beyond the gate follow the lane that soon enters **Ingleton**.

⑦ Bear right, through the houses and back into the centre of the village, bearing left to pass under the **railway viaduct** and back to the car park.

WHAT TO LOOK FOR ⓘ
Once growing in profusion in the area, the **Lady's Slipper orchid** is one of the rarest of Britain's endangered plants. They died out largely because of people digging them up to plant in their gardens, or taking the flowers for their collections of pressed specimens. English Nature has now reintroduced this beautiful plant, which has large maroon-coloured flowers, with a yellow lip and red spots inside – resembling the footwear that gives it its common name. Its leaves are pale green, with definite ribs to them. It is a characteristic plant of open woodland like that beside the waterfalls. Seeds were propagated at Kew Gardens, and the seedlings were planted in a protected area.

Erratic Progress

From Austwick along ancient tracks to see the famous Norber Erratics.

•DISTANCE•	5½ miles (8.8km)
•MINIMUM TIME•	2hrs 30min
•ASCENT / GRADIENT•	558ft (170m) ▲▲ ▲▲ ▲
•LEVEL OF DIFFICULTY•	🚶🚶 🚶🚶 🚶
•PATHS•	Field and moorland paths, tracks, lanes on return, 10 stiles
•LANDSCAPE•	Farmland and limestone upland
•SUGGESTED MAP•	aqua3 OS Explorer OL2 Yorkshire Dales – Southern & Western
•START / FINISH•	Grid reference: SD 767684
•DOG FRIENDLINESS•	Dogs should be on leads
•PARKING•	Roadside parking in Austwick village
•PUBLIC TOILETS•	None on route
•CONTRIBUTOR•	David Winpenny

BACKGROUND TO THE WALK

There is nothing showy about Austwick village. A pleasant, grey-built village, it has several old cottages, many of them dated in the traditional Dales way by a decorative lintel above the main door, showing the initials of the couple who had it built, together with the year they moved in. They mostly date from around the end of the 17th century. On the green in the centre is the restored market cross. The market itself, lost centuries ago to nearby Clapham, has not been restored.

Robin Proctor and Nappa

The walk takes you up Town Head Lane and across fields into Thwaite Lane. To your left is the ridge of limestone called Robin Proctor's Scar, named after a local farmer whose horse was trained to bring him home after a long night spent in the local pub. One night, too drunk to tell, he mounted the wrong horse and it plunged over the crag with the farmer on its back. The area below the scar was formerly a tarn, and is now home to a wide variety of marsh plants. Nappa Scar, which the walk passes after you have visited the Norber Erratics, is on the North Craven Fault line. The path goes along a ledge below a steep cliff. In the cliff wall you can see the different strata of rock, including mixed conglomerate and limestone.

The Norber Erratics are world-famous. To geologists they are a place of pilgrimage, and even the non-specialist can tell that something odd is going on here. When you arrive on the plateau above Nappa Scar, you find an extensive grass-covered area, with the remnants of a limestone pavement poking through the tufts. Strewn all over the pavement are grey boulders, some of them of huge size, perched on limestone plinths. These are the erratics. Blocks of ancient greywacke stone, they were carried here from Crummackdale, more than half a mile (800m) away, by the power of a glacier, and dumped when the ice retreated. Over the centuries, the elements have worn down the limestone pavement on which they stand – except where the erratics protected it, resulting in their elevated position.

After you cross Crummack Lane and walk though fields with a limestone ridge and ancient agricultural enclosures, you will reach Austwick Beck, where the water is crossed by

Walk 20

an ancient clapper bridge – flat stones laid across the stream from bank to bank. This leads into a walled lane that takes you to the hamlet of Wharfe. The route returns to Austwick along other walled lanes. These are the remains of old monastic ways that linked the granges, high on the fells, to the monasteries like Fountains Abbey which owned the vast sheep walks.

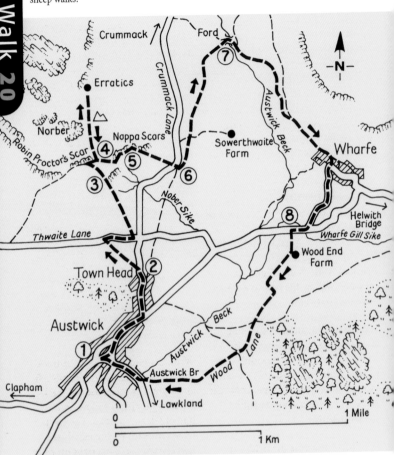

Walk 20 **Directions**

① From the triangular green in the centre of the **Austwick** village, walk northwards out of the village, following the signpost to **Horton in Ribblesdale**. Pass the **Game Cock Inn** and, just past a cottage called **Hob's Gate**, turn left up **Town Head Lane**. Just after the road bends round to the right, go left over a waymarked ladder stile.

② Walk through the field to another stile, and on to another stile on to a lane. Turn right. Just before reaching a metalled road, turn left over a ladder stile and follow the line of the track. As the track veers left, go straight on, following the line of the stone wall to a stone stile by a gate.

③ Go through the gate and continue along the rocky track. Where the stone wall on your left

WHILE YOU'RE THERE

Clapham village, which stole Austwick's market, has a beck flowing through its centre, and is surrounded by attractive woodland. The village blacksmith at the end of the 18th century was James Faraday, father of the scientist Michael Faraday. From here, too, came the botanist Reginald Farrer, whose name appears in the Latin names of many of the plant species he discovered.

bends left, by a very large boulder across the path, go right on a track to pass the right-hand edge of the scar. When you reach a signpost, go left, signposted '**Norber**'.

④ Follow the path uphill, to the plateau, and explore the **Norber Erratics**. Return the same way, back to the signpost. Turn left, following the sign to **Crummack**. Follow the track as it winds downhill then up beside a wall by the scar to a stone stile on your right.

⑤ Descend to another stile and follow the path beneath a rocky outcrop, which goes downhill with a wall to the left to reach a ladder stile on to a metalled lane. Cross the lane and go over another ladder stile opposite.

⑥ Turn left across the field. Go over two ladder stiles, cross a farm track and go over a ridge of rock to a stone stile then a ladder stile. Go over the stile and on to the track. Turn right and cross the ford on a clapper bridge.

⑦ Follow the track between the walls for ½ mile (800m) into **Wharfe**. Turn left by the bridleway sign in the village, then follow the road round to the right and go down the village approach road to reach a metalled road. Turn right. After 100yds (91m) turn left at a bridleway sign to **Wood Lane**, down the road to **Wood End Farm**.

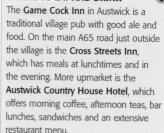

WHERE TO EAT AND DRINK

The **Game Cock Inn** in Austwick is a traditional village pub with good ale and food. On the main A65 road just outside the village is the **Cross Streets Inn**, which has meals at lunchtimes and in the evening. More upmarket is the **Austwick Country House Hotel**, which offers morning coffee, afternoon teas, bar lunches, sandwiches and an extensive restaurant menu.

⑧ By the farm buildings the track goes right. Follow it as it bends left and right to a crossroads of tracks. Go straight ahead, following the line of telegraph poles. The track winds to reach the metalled lane into the village. Turn right over the bridge to the village centre.

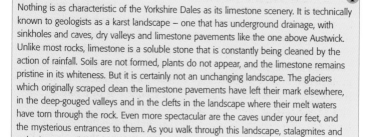

WHAT TO LOOK FOR

Nothing is as characteristic of the Yorkshire Dales as its limestone scenery. It is technically known to geologists as a karst landscape – one that has underground drainage, with sinkholes and caves, dry valleys and limestone pavements like the one above Austwick. Unlike most rocks, limestone is a soluble stone that is constantly being cleaned by the action of rainfall. Soils are not formed, plants do not appear, and the limestone remains pristine in its whiteness. But it is certainly not an unchanging landscape. The glaciers which originally scraped clean the limestone pavements have left their mark elsewhere, in the deep-gouged valleys and in the clefts in the landscape where their melt waters have torn through the rock. Even more spectacular are the caves under your feet, and the mysterious entrances to them. As you walk through this landscape, stalagmites and stalactites are still being formed beneath your feet.

Forces of Nature at Catrigg and Stainforth

From an attractive, stone-built village in the heart of the Ribble Valley, with a visit to two impressive waterfalls.

•DISTANCE•	4¾ miles (7.7km)
•MINIMUM TIME•	2hrs
•ASCENT / GRADIENT•	525ft (160m) ▲▲▲
•LEVEL OF DIFFICULTY•	👫 👫 👫
•PATHS•	Green lanes, field and riverside paths, some road, 15 stiles
•LANDSCAPE•	Moorland, farmland and river meadows with two waterfalls
•SUGGESTED MAP•	aqua3 OS Explorer OL2 Yorkshire Dales – Southern & Western
•START / FINISH•	Grid reference: SD 821672
•DOG FRIENDLINESS•	Can be off lead in walled section up to Catrigg Force
•PARKING•	Pay-and-display car park in Stainforth, just off B6479
•PUBLIC TOILETS•	At car park
•CONTRIBUTOR•	David Winpenny

BACKGROUND TO THE WALK

Stainforth is set along the Stainforth Beck as it rushes to join the River Ribble. It provides the starting point for many tracks across the moors to the east, once important routes for trade, that crossed the beck at first on the stone ford (which is what 'Stainforth' means) and later by the 14th-century bridge. The walk follows one of these ancient ways, the walled Goat Lane, as far as the path down to Catrigg Force. This spectacular waterfall, hidden in a wooded valley, was one of the favourite places of the composer Edward Elgar, who regularly stayed with his friend Dr Charles Buck in nearby Settle. Elgar would walk here, perhaps mulling over his latest work as he did so. Towards the end of the walk you pass another waterfall, Stainforth Force, where the Ribble passes over a series of limestone steps in tumultuous cascades. Just above is an attractive humpback bridge leading to Little Stainforth. The bridge was a vital link on a packhorse route between Lancaster and Ripon.

Saving the Pavement

After Catrigg Force, the walk route winds, after superb views towards Fountains Fell, towards the farms at Winskill. On the moorland just above are the Winskill Stones, pedestals of limestone topped with slate deposited here by ice-age glaciers. The slate protected the limestone beneath from the erosion that has worn down the surrounding rock. An area of limestone pavement here is now a nature reserve, but was for many years quarried for ornamental garden rocks. After a campaign to prevent this destruction, 64 acres (26ha) was purchased from the owner for £200,000. Now the area, with its rare limestone plants, is preserved; it is dedicated to the memory of television gardener Geoff Hamilton, who was patron of the appeal that raised the funds to buy the land.

Sir Isaac Newton often came to Langcliffe Hall, which has an odd door surround probably carved by the same masons who worked on the much more elaborate house in

Settle known as The Folly. Newton was friendly with the local landowners, the Paleys. One of the family, William Paley, wrote a famous book, *Evidences of Christianity* (1794). Also in Langcliffe is a former inn called the Naked Woman – a counterpart of the better-known Naked Man in Settle. If you're lucky enough to be in Langcliffe during a wedding, linger for a while to see an old Dales custom; while the ceremony takes place in the church, the village children tie up the churchyard gates and refuse to let the newly-married couple out until the guests have thrown money to them.

Walk 21 Directions

① From the car park turn right, then right again, signed 'Settle'. Over the bridge, go left through a gap in the wall. Follow the beck to an open area. Go through the white posts and turn left. Go right of the green, then turn right. Go uphill on the lane for ¾ mile (1.2km) to a gate

and ladder stile. (To visit **Catrigg Force**, take the smaller gate to the left. Return to the same point.)

② Go over the ladder stile. The track bends right. Go over a stile in a crossing wall, then turn right, signed 'Winskill'. The path bears left to join a track. Go over a stile and continue to the **farmhouses**, then go straight ahead over a stile signed

'Stainforth and Langcliffe'. As the track bends right, go left over a stile signed 'Langcliffe'.

③ Cross the field to a stone stile, turning right immediately afterwards, to follow the path downhill. After a short walled section, the path descends more steeply to a hand gate, then bears left halfway down the hill, to descend to a hand gate. Follow the path beyond to another gate.

WHERE TO EAT AND DRINK
The **Craven Heifer** in Stainforth attracts visitors from far and wide – including the Prince of Wales, who launched an initiative called 'The Pub is the Hub' here in December 2001 aimed at keeping village pubs open as a focus for the community. Apart from serving Thwaites beer and meals the Craven Heifer also doubles as a village shop.

④ After the gate the lane becomes walled. At a crossroads of paths near the village go straight on. At **Langcliffe**'s main street turn right and walk to the main road.

⑤ Cross the road and go through a gap in the wall diagonally right. Follow the footpath over a railway footbridge. Where the path ends go towards the mill. Just before the buildings take a signed path right,

WHILE YOU'RE THERE
Visit **Victoria Cave** east of Langcliffe. Nearly 1,500ft (457m) above sea level, the cave was discovered in 1838 (the year of Queen Victoria's coronation). Archaeologists revealed occupation by Roman, Celtic and Stone-Age people, as well as animals – arctic foxes and reindeer – from the ice age, and, in its earliest layers, hyenas and their prey, including elephants and woolly hippos.

going behind the mill and beside the **millpond**. Go through a gate and continue along the pond side and through a stone stile to reach a gate on the left by houses.

⑥ Go through the gate and turn right between the rows of cottages. Where the row ends, before the post box, go left over a footbridge over the **River Ribble** and at the end turn right, beside the weir, to a stone stile signed 'Stainforth'. Follow the riverside path, going over six more stiles to a **caravan site**.

⑦ Go right of the site, on the riverside path, past **Stainforth Force** to the humpback **Stainforth Bridge**. Go through a stile on to the lane, turn right over the bridge and follow the narrow lane as it bends and climbs to the main road. Turn right and take the second turning left back to the car park.

WHAT TO LOOK FOR
Stainforth Scar, seen from the riverside path in the latter part of the walk, is not a natural limestone cliffs but the remains of a quarry, now being reclaimed by nature. The history of quarrying in the Yorkshire Dales National Park goes back long before 1954 when it achieved special status; Ribblesdale especially has many quarries, some still active. More than 4 million tons of stone are quarried from the National Park each year, mainly for road building or for use in the construction industry. Quarrying is a quandary in the Park. It provides local jobs in an area where they are scarce. Many of the permissions to quarry are long standing and have many years to run – paying compensation is not an option. But conservationists argue that destroying an irreplaceable resource is not sensible, even though the companies make great efforts to clean up and plant trees as quarrying finishes. It is a complex problem, and will not easily be resolved.

Over from Littondale

From unspoiled Arncliffe to Kettlewell, and back by the River Skirfare.

•**DISTANCE**•	6½ miles (10.4km)
•**MINIMUM TIME**•	3hrs 30min
•**ASCENT / GRADIENT**•	1,315ft (400m) ▲▲▲
•**LEVEL OF DIFFICULTY**•	林 林 林
•**PATHS**•	Mostly clear, some rocky sections; may be muddy, 23 stiles
•**LANDSCAPE**•	Rocky hillside, moorland and meadows
•**SUGGESTED MAP**•	aqua3 OS Explorer OL30 Yorkshire Dales – Northern & Central
•**START / FINISH**•	Grid reference: SD 932719
•**DOG FRIENDLINESS**•	On leads – sheep in fields and on moorland
•**PARKING**•	In Arncliffe, near church
•**PUBLIC TOILETS**•	In Kettlewell (just off route)
•**CONTRIBUTOR**•	David Winpenny

BACKGROUND TO THE WALK

The village of Arncliffe and the limestone scars surrounding it may look familiar to long-time followers of the television soap opera *Emmerdale*, for the opening titles for many years featured views of the village, and in the programme's very early days it was used as a film location. The cameras have long departed, leaving visitors space to appreciate Arncliffe's spectacular setting. Great limestone scars – once the home to eagles who gave the village its name – line the hillsides all around, and the fells are riddled with caves and gulleys. Arncliffe sits on a great spit of gravel, above the floodplain of the River Skirfare. Before the building of the bridge, a ford allowed travellers an easy crossing for the many ancient tracks that converge here. Some of the tracks may be prehistoric; there is evidence south of the village of Celtic field systems and stone enclosures.

Flodden and a Challenging Cleric

St Oswald's Church may have been Saxon in origin, but nothing remains of that or its Norman successor. The tower is 15th century, while the rest was rebuilt in both the 18th and 19th centuries. The village records stretch back a long way however; the church retains a list of 34 men from the parish who went north from here in 1513 to fight the Scots at the Battle of Flodden – some of their names are still held by village families. In the churchyard is a simple stone memorial to John Robinson, Bishop of Woolwich, who caused a theological stir with his book *Honest to God*, first published in 1963. In Bridge House, close by, Charles Kingsley wrote part of *The Water Babies* – his Vendale is Littondale. Arncliffe's houses, built of local stone, are set informally around the church and the green. There is some suggestion that it may have been initially a planned village, set here by monks who were clearing people off the surrounding land so that farming could be carried out more profitably.

Leaving Arncliffe, you will almost immediately begin the long climb up the hillside to Park Scar. The path passes through a patch of ancient woodland, Byre Bank Wood, which has regenerated itself with little management or felling for centuries, because of its precarious foothold on a steep bank. There are rare plants and flowers to be found among the trees. The descent to Kettlewell will take you through The Slit, a dramatic, narrow cleft in the limestone rocks above the village, while approach to Hawkswick gives wide views over Littondale, much of which is a conservation area. The fields are managed as wildflower meadows that provide winter fodder for the cattle. Littondale is also a must for ornithologists – look out on the walk for curlews, peregrine falcons and redshanks, as well as dippers, oystercatchers and yellow wagtails.

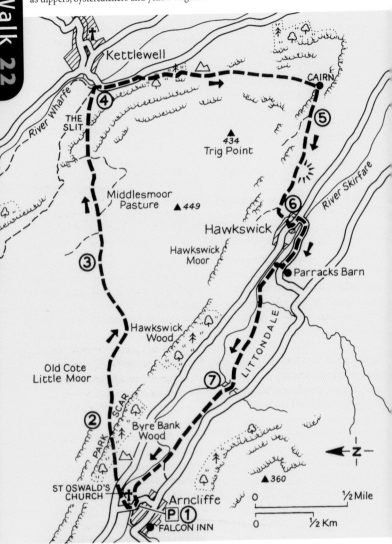

Walk 22 Directions

① From the car park, cross the bridge and turn right at its end, over a gated stile. Walk parallel with the river and go up steps to cross the road via two stiles. Bear right and follow the footpath steeply uphill over a stile and through a gate. Bear right and climb through the woods up **Park Scar** to a stile.

WHERE TO EAT AND DRINK ⓘ

For an authentic Dales experience, visit the **Falcon Inn** in Arncliffe, run by the same family for four generations. Here you'll be served good beer direct from the barrel. There are no pumps, pot jugs are filled at the barrel and the ale is poured from them into your glass. The Falcon also serves home-cooked food – they prefer notice of vegetarians!

② Beyond, follow the footpath to the right to another ladder stile. Pass a signpost and go through a gap in a tumbled wall to another signpost. Continue to a ladder stile, then cross the corner of the field to another ladder stile at the summit.

③ Beyond the stile, bear half right and descend to a ladder stile. Follow the path beyond towards Kettlewell, descending steeply to a signpost. Cross a track to reach a limestone scar. Descend through a narrow cleft (**The Slit**), then walk down to a stile and, beyond it, a footpath sign. Turn right, go through a gate and on to the road.

④ Turn right for 300yds (274m), then go right through a gate signed 'Hawkswick', bending right again at another sign. Climb through

WHAT TO LOOK FOR ⓘ

Take some time to explore the ancient village of **Kettlewell**. Its name means the stream in a narrow valley – the village is built alongside the Dowber Gill Beck as it tumbles into the River Wharfe. Towering over Kettlewell are the long ridges of limestone and the huge bulk of Great Whernside. A weekly market used to be held at Kettlewell, which was on one of the main coaching routes from London to the North – beyond the village the route went over into Coverdale and into Richmond. Three inns served the travellers, and now provide for the many tourists who flock here.

woodland, go through a waymarked gate, then bear left through a gap in the wall. Continue uphill, winding steeply to a gap in a wall beside a stile. Bear left to another stile then ascend the grassy path, bearing right where the path forks, to another stile. Beyond, continue downhill bending right by a **cairn**.

⑤ At a junction of tracks continue with a wall on your left. Go through a gated stile and into **Hawkswick** village. Bear left at the junction, curve right between buildings and go through a gate to the bridge.

WHILE YOU'RE THERE ⓘ

Explore further up Littondale. The village of Litton is sited where the valley narrows, while beyond is the hamlet of **Halton Gill**. An 18th-century curate here, the Revd Miles Wilson, wrote a book to explain astronomy to ordinary folk. In *The Man in the Moon* he imagines a cobbler climbing to the moon from the top of Pen-y-ghent, then wandering at will around the solar system.

⑥ Cross and follow the road, bending right. Just before farm buildings on the left, turn right towards the footbridge; do not cross, but turn left at the 'Arncliffe' sign. Follow the river, going over three stiles, then a footbridge and another ladder stile. The path leaves the riverside and reaches a gate. Cross the field beyond to a ladder stile, then another footbridge.

⑦ Walk to the right of the barn and go through a gate, then bear left to a squeeze stile in a crossing wall. Cross a track and go through three more stiles, following the river, to go through a gate near a house. Follow the waymarked posts to a kissing gate and past the **churchyard** to the starting point.

Walk 23

Scar House and Nidderdale

A walk in Upper Nidderdale, with natural and artificial landscapes.

•DISTANCE•	8¼ miles (13.3km)
•MINIMUM TIME•	3hrs 30min
•ASCENT / GRADIENT•	886ft (270m) ▲▲ ▲
•LEVEL OF DIFFICULTY•	🚶🚶 🚶🚶 🚶🚶
•PATHS•	Moorland tracks, field paths and lanes, 16 stiles
•LANDSCAPE•	High hills of Upper Nidderdale, farmland and riverside
•SUGGESTED MAP•	aqua3 OS Explorer 298 Nidderdale or OS Explorer OL30 Yorkshire Dales – Northern & Central
•START / FINISH•	Grid reference: SE 070766
•DOG FRIENDLINESS•	Can be off leads on moorland, on lead in farmland
•PARKING•	Signed car park at top of reservoir access road
•PUBLIC TOILETS•	By car park
•CONTRIBUTOR•	David Winpenny

BACKGROUND TO THE WALK

Opened in 1936, Scar House is one of a string of reservoirs in Nidderdale that serve the city of Bradford, 30 miles (48km) to the south – the others include Angram, to the west, and Gouthwaite, down towards Pateley Bridge. It is still possible to see evidence around the dam of the remains of the village in which the navvies who built it lived and of the ancillary buildings where they stored machinery and dressed the stone. There were some protests before the dams were built about the drowning of parts of the valley, and rumours that Nidderdale was left out of the Yorkshire Dales National Park when it was designated in 1954 because the reservoirs had blighted the landscape. Redress was made in 1994 when 603 square miles (1562sq km) of Nidderdale became an Area of Outstanding Natural Beauty.

How Stean Gorge

'Yorkshire's Little Switzerland' says the publicity for How Stean Gorge. The How Stean Beck has forced its way through the limestone here, cutting a gorge up to 80ft (25m) deep, with pools and overhangs enough to please both geologists and small children. Lichen and moss cling to the rock walls, and trees overhang it precariously. For a fee, you can enter the gorge, crossing and re-crossing by footbridges and exploring the narrow paths. The more adventurous can borrow a torch to investigate the deep Tom Taylor's Cave, said to be named after a highwayman who holed up here.

The village of Middlesmoor, visible after passing How Stean Gorge, is one of the most dramatically-sited in the area. Set high on a bluff of the hills overlooking the Nidd Valley, its 19th-century church is on the site of a building thought to have been founded by St Chad; it contains the head of a Saxon cross. One of the most notorious of Victorian murderers, Eugene Aram, who killed his wife's lover and was hanged when the body came to light 14 years later, was married here. Following the Nidderdale Way from Lofthouse, you may well see groups donning caving gear. They are likely to be preparing to enter the Goyden Pot system, 3½ miles (5.8km) of underground caves and passages cut through the limestone by the River Nidd. An early guide book noted that 'Goyden Pot Hole is a large Rock, into which the River Nidd enters by an arch finely formed… with a lighted candle a person may walk three hundred yards into it with safety.' This procedure is not recommended today! Goyden Pot connects with Manchester Hole, a little further upstream, where the river may also disappear; the riverbed above is frequently dry.

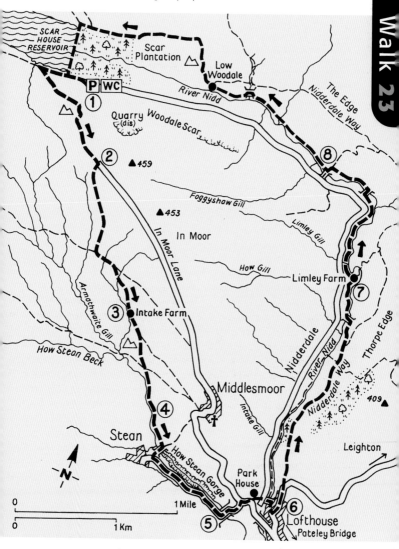

Walk 23 **Directions**

① Walk towards the dam wall and continue along the left side of the reservoir to a **Nidderdale Way** signpost, just before a gate. Follow the track left uphill. The track levels and goes through a gate. A few paces beyond, go right through a gate in the wall.

② Go diagonally towards the wall on your right, then follow a faint path it as it bends left. At a track turn left, go over two cattle grids

Walk 23

and turn right through the field towards a gate in a crossing hedge. Walk down the next field and pass between farm buildings, following the waymark, to a gate.

③ Cross the field to a handgate by the barn. Pass to the right of a wall to reach a wooden stile. Continue through woodland, ascending left to a waymark, then along the hillside to a stile, where you descend to the riverside path.

④ Go through a squeeze stile, and where the path divides take the left-hand fork, away from the wire fence. Ascend to a ladder stile, then to a stone stile by a **Nidderdale Way** sign. Turn right, go through a gate and cross a footbridge. Ascend the steps to two more stiles on to a lane. Turn left down the lane, passing **How Stean Gorge** entrance, to a stone bridge.

> ### WHERE TO EAT AND DRINK ⓘ
> The **Crown Hotel** in Lofthouse does substantial bar meals at lunchtime and in the evenings, and serves good Yorkshire beer. The **How Stean Gorge café** has a very good local reputation and an extensive menu; the raspberry pavlova is a special favourite!

⑤ Go left over the bridge, and turn right at the T-junction, signed 'Lofthouse'. Where the road bends right, go ahead to a gate and to the right of the buildings. Go through another gate, across the road and ahead over the bridge. Turn right and pass between buildings to reach the village street.

⑥ Turn left and climb the hill. As the road bends right, go left down a grassy track to a gate. Continue along the lower track through four gates, then follow the waymarks to

> ### WHAT TO LOOK FOR ⓘ
> The **red kite**, once a familiar sight all over England, was hunted almost to extinction in the 19th century. It has now been reintroduced in Yorkshire, and the birds have been seen over-wintering in Upper Nidderdale. They have flown in from their nesting sites on the Harewood Estate, near Leeds, or from Scotland. Their long, angled wings and translucent forked tails make them distinctive. Mature birds have rusty-red plumage, with white feathers around the head.

the riverbank. Cross the river to another gate, and continue along the bank, over two stiles to a gate. Turn right towards the farm.

⑦ Just after the first buildings on your left, go through a gateway, through another gate and on to a riverside path. Follow the path over two stiles to a footbridge with a stile at its end. Cross over and turn left to continue along the riverside, going through a gate and over a stile to reach a gate on to a track.

⑧ Turn left over the cattle grid, then right just before a bridge. Where the track bends right, go ahead through four stiles to a gate. Cross a stream to another gate and follow the fence down to a field. Go through a waymarked gate to pass between buildings to another gate. The track climbs right and goes through five gates, turning towards the dam and descending to a track. Turn right and go through a gate. The track becomes metalled. Cross the dam back to the car park.

> ### WHILE YOU'RE THERE ⓘ
> Nidderdale is highly regarded for its **fishing**. If you want to fish in Scar House reservoir – mainly for trout and grayling – you can obtain a ticket from the post offices in Lofthouse or Pateley Bridge.

Spectacular Landscapes in Limestone Country

The noble Malham Cove is the highlight of this quintessential Dales walk.

•DISTANCE•	6¼ miles (10.1km)
•MINIMUM TIME•	3hrs
•ASCENT / GRADIENT•	1,148ft (350m) ▲▲▲
•LEVEL OF DIFFICULTY•	🚶🚶 🚶🚶 🚶
•PATHS•	Well-marked field and moorland paths, more than 400 steps in descent from Malham Cove, 5 stiles
•LANDSCAPE•	Spectacular limestone country, including Malham Cove
•SUGGESTED MAP•	aqua3 OS Explorer OL30 Yorkshire Dales – Northern & Central
•START / FINISH•	Grid reference: SD 894658
•DOG FRIENDLINESS•	Mostly off lead, except where sheep are present or signs indicate otherwise
•PARKING•	At Water Sinks, near gateway across road
•PUBLIC TOILETS•	Car park in Malham village
•CONTRIBUTOR•	David Winpenny

BACKGROUND TO THE WALK

As you begin this walk, the stream from Malham Tarn suddenly disappears in a tumble of rocks. This is the aptly-named Water Sinks. In spectacular limestone country like this, it is not unusual for streams to plunge underground – it was subterranean watercourses that sculpted the cave systems beneath your feet. As you will see as you continue, this particular stream has not always been so secretive. The now-dry valley of Watlowes just beyond Water Sinks was formed by water action. It was this stream, in fact, that produced Malham Cove, and once fell over its spectacular cliff in a waterfall 230ft (70m) high. Although in very wet weather the stream goes a little further than Water Sinks, it is 200 years since water reached the cove.

Pavement and Cove

Beyond Watlowes valley you reach a stretch of limestone pavement – not the biggest, but probably the best-known example of this unusual phenomenon in the Dales. The natural fissures in the rock have been enlarged by millennia of rain and frost, forming the characteristic blocks, called clints, and the deep clefts, called grikes. It's worth looking closely into the grikes; their sheltered environment provides a home to spleenworts and ferns, and you will sometimes find rare primulas flowering in their shade. The limestone pavement is the summit of the most spectacular of natural features in the Yorkshire Dales – the huge sweep of the cliffs known as Malham Cove. Take care as you explore the pavement, as the edge is not fenced. As you descend the 400-plus steps, the sheer scale of the cove becomes apparent; 230ft (70m) high, it was formed by a combination of glacial action, earth movement (it is on the line of the Middle Craven Fault) and the biting away of its lip by the former waterfall.

Fields, Falls and Fairies

On the slopes to the east of Malham Cove you can see ancient terraced fields. Up to 200yds (183m) long, they were painstakingly cut and levelled by Anglian farmers in the 8th century for producing crops. They show how the population was expanding then, and that there was simply not enough farmland on the valley floors to feed everyone. After walking through Malham village, the route passes through fields and a wooded gorge – called Little Gordale – to Janet's Foss. One of the classic waterfalls of the Dales, it is noted for the screen of tufa, a soft, porous limestone curtain formed by deposits from the stream, that now lies over the original lip of stone that was responsible for creating the fall. Janet (or Jennett) was the Queen of the local fairies, and is said to have lived in the cave behind the fall.

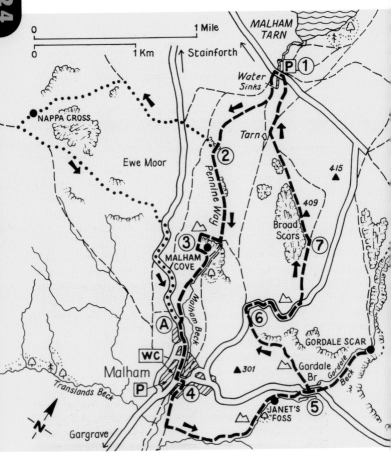

Walk 24 Directions

① From the car parking space, walk through the gate, then turn left through the kissing gate at the **Malham Cove** sign. Walk parallel with the dry-stone wall on your left

and follow the dry valley as it bends to reach a stile at the head of another dry valley.

② Turn left and follow the footpath down the valley to reach a stile at the end. Go over the stile, then walk straight ahead to the limestone pavement at the top of **Malham Cove**. Turn right and walk along the pavement to reach steps. Take great care here, both of the sheer drop down to your left and the gaps in the limestone pavement (known as grikes). Turn left to descend cautiously more than 400 steps to the foot of the **cove**.

③ When you reach the bottom turn right along the track beside the river. Go through two kissing gates to reach the road. Turn left and follow the road into the centre of **Malham** village. Turn left to go over the bridge.

> ### WHERE TO EAT AND DRINK ⓘ
> As one of the most visited villages of the Yorkshire Dales, Malham is well-supplied with eating places. The **Malham Café** offers meals and snacks, while the **Buck Inn** has good pub meals and fine beer. The **Lister Arms Hotel** provides good food, real ale and, in summer, real cider.

④ Turn right along the side of the river on a track, following the signs marked '**Janet's Foss**'. Follow the signposted, mostly gravelled, path through eight gates. Eventually the footpath climbs up through woodland and passes beside the waterfall (Janet's Foss) to a kissing gate. Turn right along the road, towards **Gordale Scar**.

⑤ At the bridge go through a gate to the left. (To visit **Gordale Scar**, continue straight ahead here. Take a signed gate to the left and follow

> ### WHILE YOU'RE THERE ⓘ
> Visit **Gordale Scar** (a short walk beyond Janet's Foss). The route takes you along a valley that narrows and twists beneath cliffs, until a final bend brings you to the waterfall in the narrowest part of the gorge. Once thought to be a collapsed cave system, it is now believed to have been formed by erosion from the stream, which has carved this spectacular gash through the limestone.

the path up through a field into the gorge. Keep going on the obvious route as far as the waterfall and then follow the same route back to the bridge.) On the main route, follow the signed public footpath uphill through two stiles and out on to a lane.

⑥ Turn right and walk uphill for ¼ mile (400m), to a ladder stile over the wall on your left. Follow the track, going left at a fork to reach another footpath fingerpost.

⑦ Turn left, following the sign, to reach a small tarn. Turn right at the sign for **Malham Tarn**, go over a ladder stile, take the left-hand path and follow it back to the car park.

Extending the Walk

You can avoid the steep descent by Malham Cove by taking a scenic extension to this walk, across the limestone uplands to **Nappa Cross** from Point ② and descending to **Malham** along an old drove road which joins a minor road to rejoin the main route at Point Ⓐ.

> ### WHAT TO LOOK FOR ⓘ
> Nothing is what is seems in the Alice-in-Wonderland world around Malham. The logical among us would assume that if water disappears underground, heading in the direction of Malham Cove, just a mile (1.6km) ahead, it will reappear at the base of the Cove. But logic is wrong. The stream that bubbles up from under Malham Cove actually comes from Smelt Mill Sink, ¾ mile (1.2km) to the west of Water Sinks. The stream from Water Sinks, on the other hand, reappears at Aire Head Springs to become the infant River Aire.

Walk 25

The Monks' Road and Bordley

Remote farmsteads and an old walled green lane between Malhamdale and Wharfedale.

•DISTANCE•	5 miles (8km)
•MINIMUM TIME•	2hrs
•ASCENT / GRADIENT•	436ft (133m) ▲ ▲ ▲
•LEVEL OF DIFFICULTY•	🚶🚶 🚶🚶 🚶🚶
•PATHS•	Tracks and field paths. 2 stiles
•LANDSCAPE•	Moorland and farmland
•SUGGESTED MAP•	aqua3 OS Explorer OL2 Yorkshire Dales – Southern & Western
•START / FINISH•	Grid reference: SD 951652
•DOG FRIENDLINESS•	On leads – sheep on moorland and livestock in fields
•PARKING•	Roadside parking, before gate across lane from Skirethorns
•PUBLIC TOILETS•	None on route
•CONTRIBUTOR•	David Winpenny

BACKGROUND TO THE WALK

Many places in the Yorkshire Dales can be described as 'remote' – and Bordley must be one of the least accessible. No metalled roads lead to it, and the settlement (really only a hamlet of a couple of farmhouses) is almost invisible from most of the surrounding countryside, lying as it does in a secluded hollow of the hills. Although the buildings are mostly 18th and 19th century, Bordley has a long, if uneventful, history. It is mentioned in Domesday Book as Borelaie, and its Old English name may mean 'the wood from which the boards were taken' – or perhaps 'the woodland clearing belonging to Brorda'. Whichever it is, the woods have long since gone, and this is now moorland country, some of it enclosed and improved in the 18th century for agriculture. Around Bordley there is evidence of even older settlement. Mastiles Lane ploughs through the middle of a Roman camp a little way to the west, while the east, just off the road up from Skirethorns, is evidence of a prehistoric field system.

Mastiles and the Monks

The early part of the walk takes you to Mastiles Gate, one of the landmarks along Mastiles Lane, a superb green track that for centuries has linked Wharfedale and Malhamdale. Its origins were monastic; the monks of Fountains Abbey near Ripon needed straightforward access to their vast estates in the southern parts of the Yorkshire Dales and in the Lake District. So, like the Romans before them, they constructed long roads directly over the fells. The route over Kilnsey Moor was marked by crosses – the bases of some survive along the route. The monastic route crossed the River Wharfe by a wooden bridge at Kilnsey, and then went on to Ripon along the route of what is now the B6265 via Pateley Bridge.

In the 18th and 19th centuries Mastiles Lane was used as a drove road, when great herds of cattle were driven along the lane to market. There was a regular sale at Great Close, near Malham Tarn, where up to 5,000 cattle, most of them from Scotland, were regularly sold. It was at this time that the lane received its walls, to prevent the cattle straying.

Tarmac Outcry

In the early 1960s plans were put forward to tarmac Mastiles Lane so that traffic would be able to drive from Malham into Wharfedale. A public outcry quickly saw the idea abandoned and the route is still a haven of peace for walkers and riders – though more recently there has been further controversy, this time about the use of such green lanes by four-wheel drive off-road vehicles, which can cause damage.

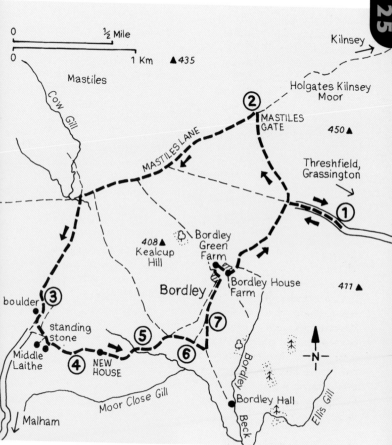

Walk 25 **Directions**

① From the parking place go through the gate and follow the metalled lane downhill to a crossroad of tracks. Turn right here, signposted 'Kilnsey'. Follow the track parallel with the dry-stone wall on your right to reach a crossing track at another signpost. This is **Mastiles Gate**.

② Turn left along the lane signed 'Street Gate'. At the next signpost continue straight on through the gate and on to another gate. In 100yds (91m) beyond this gate turn left through a gate in the wall and follow the track with a fence on your left. The track eventually goes between walls to a gate.

③ Go through the gate and follow the track, which bears right by a large triangular boulder. After 200yds (183m), pass through a gateway and turn left, going to the left of the **bungalow** down to a large standing stone near **Middle Laithe**. Turn left through the farmyard and over a cattle grid. Follow the farm track, crossing a second cattle grid by a National Trust sign for New House farm.

WHILE YOU'RE THERE ⓘ

Visit **Kilnsey Crag** by the Wharfe where a great limestone cliff dominates the valley, with an overhanging nose that provides a severe test to climbers. The crag was formed when an ice-age glacier ground away the end of a limestone spur as it made its way south from Littondale. Once, a lake lapped the crag's foot – it silted up long ago, leaving rich farm land.

---

④ Continue along a walled lane into the farmyard of **New House**. Go through a gate then bear half right to go down the field to a gate in the bottom left-hand corner. Go through the gate, turn left and follow the line of telegraph poles. Go over a stile and descend across the stream.

⑤ Follow the path on the other side of the stream, to the right to the telegraph poles. The path eventually follows a wall on your right. Go through the first gate on your right and follow the wall on

---

WHERE TO EAT AND DRINK ⓘ

Draw a circle of 4 miles (6.4km) in diameter centred on Bordley – and you will not find a pub or café. So before or after the walk head for Grassington, which has plenty of tea shops as well as several recommended pubs including the **Foresters Arms**, or try the **Old Hall Inn** at Threshfield.

---

your left, bearing right to go through a gap in the crossing wall.

⑥ Bear left to go round the angle of the wall on your left to a stone stile in the crossing wall. Follow the wall on the left up the field, past a tumbled wall, to join a track.

⑦ Turn right along the track, going through two gates. After the second gate bend right, then go left at a blue waymark sign and through the farm buildings to double gates. Beyond the gates turn right and follow the track past the farmhouse. Climb the track, going through a gate, then descend to another gate. Turn right to the crossroads and ascend the hill back to the start.

WHAT TO LOOK FOR ⓘ

The **merlin**, Britain's smallest falcon, may sometimes be spotted above the moorland. The male has a blue-grey tail and back, while the larger female is brown-backed and has a banded tail. They most often nest on the ground, but have been known to occupy abandoned crows' nests. Like most falcons, their diet consists mainly of small mammals and insects, but more especially other birds, particularly ring ouzels and meadow pipits, which they catch in their swooping and spiralling flight.

Three Nidderdale Villages

From Lofthouse to Ramsgill and Middlesmoor in the valley of the River Nidd.

•DISTANCE•	7 miles (11.3km)
•MINIMUM TIME•	3hrs
•ASCENT / GRADIENT•	656ft (200m) ▲▲▲
•LEVEL OF DIFFICULTY•	🚶🚶 🚶🚶 🚶
•PATHS•	Mostly field paths and tracks; may be muddy, 20 stiles
•LANDSCAPE•	Rich farmland and moorland, wide views from Middlesmoor
•SUGGESTED MAP•	aqua3 OS Explorer OL30 Yorkshire Dales – Northern & Central
•START / FINISH•	Grid reference: SE 101734
•DOG FRIENDLINESS•	Can be off lead on walled section between Studfold Farm and Stean, but should be on lead for rest of walk
•PARKING•	Car park by Memorial Hall in Lofthouse
•PUBLIC TOILETS•	None on route
•CONTRIBUTOR•	David Winpenny

BACKGROUND TO THE WALK

Much of upper Nidderdale was proposed as an Area of Outstanding Natural Beauty in 1947 – but official designation happened only in 1994. There were discussions as to whether the area should be included as part of the Yorkshire Dales National Park but Nidderdale was designated separately. It is an area of moorland wildness and deep, farmed valleys. In the late 19th and 20th centuries parts of the dale were dammed as a chain of reservoirs – Angram, Scar House and Gouthwaite – was constructed to supply water to the city of Bradford.

Monks, Fairies and a Murderer

Throughout Nidderdale are small, stone-built settlements like those visited on the walk – many of them of considerable antiquity. The monks of Fountains Abbey, near Ripon, founded the attractive village of Lofthouse as a grange in the Middles Ages. It was one of the bases from which they controlled their vast farming interests in Nidderdale. Lofthouse today now consists mainly of 19th-century cottages. Ramsgill, at the southern end of the route, is at the head of Gouthwaite Reservoir, which was opened in 1899 and is renowned for its spectacular bird life. The village was the birthplace, in 1704, of Eugene Aram, scholar and murderer, who arranged for the slaughter of his wife's lover and was hanged in Knaresborough for the crime – a deed retold by both Bulwer Lytton and the poet Thomas Hood. The village was also used in the feature film *Fairy Tale: A True Story* (1997) about two Yorkshire girls who hoaxed many – including Arthur Conan Doyle and Harry Houdini – into believing they had photographed fairies in Cottingley near Bradford. In the third village, Middlesmoor, with its spectacular hilltop setting, the head of an Anglo-Saxon cross with its inscription to St Cedd in the church again indicates the age of a settlement which today seems to date mainly from the last two centuries.

It was once possible to travel from Pateley Bridge up the dale on Britain's only corporation-run light railway. The Nidd Valley Light Railway, originally laid as a narrow-gauge line by the builders of Angram Reservoir, was taken over by Bradford Corporation in 1907 and re-laid as standard gauge. It ran regular passenger services from Pateley Bridge (where it connected with the North Eastern Railway's line) to Lofthouse, with stations at Wath and what was called Ramsgill (but was really at Bouthwaite). It closed to passengers in 1929, but the track is still visible on much of the route.

Walk 26 Directions

① Walk downhill past the **Crown Hotel** to the main road and turn left. Just beyond **High Lofthouse farm** go right, through a stile.

Follow the track to a waymarked stile, then bear left to another stile. After it head half right to go through a gate in the field corner. Turn left, then immediately right through the next gate. Follow the fence to another stile on to a road.

② Cross the road and go through a gate. Follow the wire fence to a stile, then walk along the farm track. Before the next gateway, go left over a stile, then immediately right over another. Bear left and ascend, following the path through three gates to a track. Turn right, down through a gate. At the next junction take the right-hand track, go left of the farmhouse, though a gate and to a stile. Follow the waymarkers to a wooden gate. Bear right, go over a wooden bridge, through a metal gate and ahead. Bear right past the house to a gravelled track and a metalled road.

> ### *WHERE TO EAT AND DRINK* ℹ
> For top-of-the-range meals, the **Yorke Arms** in Ramsgill has an enviable reputation. There are also two **Crown Hotels** on or near the route, one in Lofthouse and another in Middlesmoor.

track joins from the left, turn right. At the bottom, bend left above the houses and descend in to **Stean**.

⑥ The track becomes metalled. Bear right, pass the telephone box, then take a stile on the left signed 'Middlesmoor'. Go through another stile, down steps, over a bridge and up steps. After the gate at the top, follow signs through three stiles on to the road. Turn left towards Middlesmoor. Near the hilltop turn right beside the **Wesleyan chapel** to the gateway of the parish church.

> ### *WHILE YOU'RE THERE* ℹ
> A visit to the attractive town of **Pateley Bridge** will prove rewarding. There are many fascinating small shops, as well as walks by the River Nidd and the interesting Nidderdale Museum in King Street, housed in a former workhouse.

③ Bear right down the road to a T-junction. Turn left, over the bridge. Take the next track right, by the triangular green, then bear right again signed 'Stean'. Go through a gate on to a track, and over four cattle grids to where the track bends left up to **Grindstone Hill House**.

④ Go straight on, over four stiles. At **West House Farm** go over a stile between the farm and a bungalow, cross the farm road, follow the waymarked posts and continue through two gates and over a ladder stile to descend to a signpost near a barn. Continue into a wooded valley and over a small bridge.

⑤ At a T-junction of tracks, turn left, uphill, and follow the walled track as it bends right. Beyond the farm entrance the track becomes grassy. In 100yds (91m), after a

⑦ Turn right before the gate, through a stile signed 'Lofthouse'. Go down steps then through a stile and two gateways by **Halfway House**. Continue through a stile, then go diagonally left to a gate in the corner. In the lay-by go left though a gate, then right of the buildings to another gate. Cross the lane and go over a bridge, then bear right to the centre of **Lofthouse**. Turn right to the car park.

> ### *WHAT TO LOOK FOR* ℹ
> **Oil beetles** have been sighted at Middlesmoor. Thought to be the most common of the seven species of oil beetle in Britain this was *meloë proscarabaeus*. Unlike other beetles, their wing cases do not overlap, making them look as if they are wearing waistcoats. They also have kinked antennae – the male beetle's end with blobs. Oil beetles get their name from an oily fluid they secrete from their leg joints if they're disturbed. It deters predators and can cause blistering on human skin.

Walk 27

The Mines of Greenhow and Bewerley Moor

Through a landscape of lead mining, from one of Yorkshire's highest villages.

•DISTANCE•	6 miles (9.7km)
•MINIMUM TIME•	2hrs 45min
•ASCENT / GRADIENT•	1,181ft (360m) ▲▲▲
•LEVEL OF DIFFICULTY•	🚶🚶 🚶🚶 🚶
•PATHS•	Field and moorland paths and tracks, 5 stiles
•LANDSCAPE•	Moorland and valley, remains of lead mining industry
•SUGGESTED MAP•	aqua3 OS Explorer 298 Nidderdale
•START / FINISH•	Grid reference: SE 128643
•DOG FRIENDLINESS•	Dogs can be off lead for much of route
•PARKING•	Car park at Toft Gate Lime Kiln
•PUBLIC TOILETS•	None on route
•CONTRIBUTOR•	David Winpenny

BACKGROUND TO THE WALK

It is a long haul from Pateley Bridge up Greenhow Hill to the village of Greenhow, one of the highest in Yorkshire, at around 1,300ft (396m) above sea level. Until the early 17th century this was all bleak and barren moorland. When lead mining on a significant scale developed in the area in the 1600s, a settlement was established here, though most of the surviving buildings are late 18th and 19th century. Many of the cottages also have a small piece of attached farmland, for the miners were also farmers, neither occupation alone giving them a stable income or livelihood. In a way typical of such mining villages, the church and the pub – the Miners Arms, of course – are at the very centre.

Romans and Monks

Romans are the first known miners of Greenhow, though there is said to be some evidence of even earlier activity, as far back as the Bronze Age. The Romans had a camp near Pateley Bridge, and ingots of lead – called 'pigs' – have been found near by, dating from the 1st century AD. In the Middle Ages lead from Yorkshire became important for roofing castles and cathedrals – it is said that it was even used in Jerusalem. Production was governed by the major landowners, the monasteries, and some, like Fountains and Byland, became rich from selling charters for mining and from royalties. After the monasteries were dissolved, the new landowners wanted to exploit their mineral rights, and encouraged many small-scale enterprises in return for a share of the profits.

As you leave Greenhow and begin to descend into the valley of the Gill Beck, you pass through the remains of the Cockhill Mine. It is still possible to make out the dressing floor, where the lead ore was separated from the waste rock and other minerals, and the location of the smelt works, where the ore was processed. Beyond, by the Ashfold Side Beck, were the Merryfield Mines and, where the route crosses the beck, there are extensive remains of the Prosperous Smelt Mill. All these mines were active in the middle of the 19th century, and some had a brief resurgence in the mid 20th.

Besides the Lead

The vast retaining banks of Coldstones Quarry rise above the car park at Toft Gate Lime Kiln. This enormous hole (you can see it from the viewing point at the top of the bank) opened about 1900 and produces almost 1 million tons of limestone a year. Around Greenhow the limestone layers are particularly deep, allowing large blocks to be cut. Across it run two mineral veins, called Garnet Vein and Sun Vein, both of which have been mined for lead and for fluorite. Other minerals found in smaller quantities in the rock here are barite, calcite and galena, as well as crystals of cerrusite, anglesite and occasionally quartz.

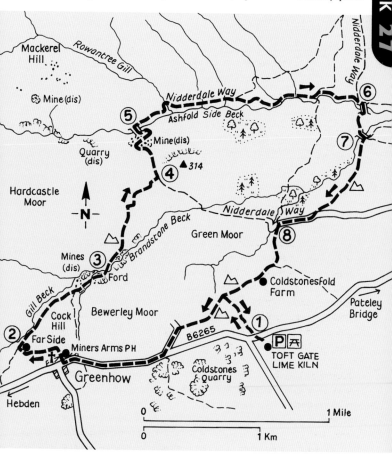

Walk 27 Directions

① Cross the road from the car park and go over the stile opposite into a field. Follow the faint path downhill, over a gate in the wall and to the right of a barn. Cross another stile and descend to the track Turn left and walk up the hill through

two gates to a road. Turn left and walk up to the main road. Turn right and follow this past the burial ground and the **Miners Arms**. About 100yds (91m) after the pub, just past a converted chapel, take a lane to the right. At the junction go left and follow the lane to a cattle grid and through a gate. Curve right, round behind the farmhouse.

Walk 27

② Follow the track downhill into the valley of **Gill Beck** and then **Brandstone Beck**, where there are the extensive remains of lead mining activity. Where the track swings left, go ahead down the valley to reach the main track near a concrete building. Go right of the building and just beyond go ahead down the valley to the ford.

③ Cross and follow the obvious track up the hill. Go over a stile beside a gate by trees then, 100yds (91m) beyond, take another stile on the right. Follow the track towards the farm, going left between stone walls, and descend to another stile on to a track.

④ Turn left and go through a waymarked gateway. By a spoil heap follow the track to the right and downhill. Veer slightly left, past an iron cogwheel, to cross **Ashfold Side Beck** on a concrete causeway to a gate.

⑤ Follow the bridleway sign to the right and climb the hill, to a **Nidderdale Way** sign, where you turn right along the track to a gate. Wind round the head of a valley through two gateways and over three cattle grids. Just beyond the third, go through a metal gate to the right and over the bridge.

⑥ Go ahead then bear left to another gate and follow the track uphill and left to a wall. Turn right at the end of the wall along a lane between stone walls. Continue along the track to a gate and cross a footbridge.

⑦ Turn right through a gate and follow the track uphill, passing through another gate. Turn left at another track, making towards the farmhouse, but bear right across the grass to meet a metalled lane. Turn right and follow the lane over a cattle grid.

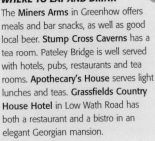

WHERE TO EAT AND DRINK

The **Miners Arms** in Greenhow offers meals and bar snacks, as well as good local beer. **Stump Cross Caverns** has a tea room. Pateley Bridge is well served with hotels, pubs, restaurants and tea rooms. **Apothecary's House** serves light lunches and teas. **Grassfields Country House Hotel** in Low Wath Road has both a restaurant and a bistro in an elegant Georgian mansion.

⑧ About 100yds (91m) beyond the farm on the right, turn left up a path. After a cattle grid turn right and follow the track through a gate. At **Coldstonesfold Farm** turn right and follow the track uphill through a gate, before turning left over the stile to retrace your outward route to return to **Toft Gate Lime Kiln**.

WHAT TO LOOK FOR

The **lime kiln** at Toft Gate is very well-preserved and is now protected by English Heritage. It was built in the 1860s to help meet the Victorians' huge demand for lime, both in agriculture and building. A path from the car park leads you round the site where the flue, chimney and main furnace are visible. You can also see inside the kiln itself and interpretive panels explain the workings.

A Medieval Walk from Fountains

From the ruins of Fountains Abbey to medieval Markenfield Hall.

•DISTANCE•	6½ miles (10.4km)
•MINIMUM TIME•	3hrs
•ASCENT / GRADIENT•	328ft (100m) ▲ ▲ ▲
•LEVEL OF DIFFICULTY•	🚶 🚶 🚶
•PATHS•	Field paths and tracks, a little road walking, 8 stiles
•LANDSCAPE•	Farmland and woodland
•SUGGESTED MAP•	aqua3 OS Explorer 298 Nidderdale
•START / FINISH•	Grid reference: SE 270681
•DOG FRIENDLINESS•	Dogs should be on leads on field paths, can be off lead in parts of woodland
•PARKING•	Car park at west end of abbey, or at visitor centre
•PUBLIC TOILETS•	Fountains Abbey visitor centre
•CONTRIBUTOR•	David Winpenny

BACKGROUND TO THE WALK

After you have climbed the hill from the car park and begun the walk along the valley side, following the ancient abbey wall, the south front of Fountains Hall is below you. Built by Sir Stephen Proctor in 1611, it is a fine Jacobean house, with lots of mullioned windows and cross gables. Were it anywhere other than at the entrance to Fountains Abbey it would be seen as one of the great houses of the age. Sir Stephen was, by all accounts, not the most scrupulous of men, having made his huge fortune as Collector of Fines on Penal Statutes. Nor did he respect the abbey buildings; the stone he built his house with was taken from the south east corner of the monastic remains.

Abbey and Abbot

A little further along the path, the abbey ruins come into view. When monks from St Mary's Abbey in York first settled here in 1132 it was a wild and desolate place. Nevertheless their abbey prospered, and became one of the country's richest and most powerful Cistercian monasteries. More remains of Fountains than of any other abbey ruin in the country. Its church was 360ft (97.5m) long. The other buildings, laid out along (and over) the River Skell, give a vivid impression of what life was like here in the Middle Ages. All came to an end in 1539 when King Henry VIII dissolved the larger monasteries. This was only a few years after Abbot Marmaduke Huby had built the huge tower, a symbol of what he believed was the enduring power of his abbey.

Mr Aislabie's Garden

Beyond Fountains Abbey are the pleasure gardens laid out between 1716 and 1781 by John Aislabie and his son William. John had retired to his estate here at Studley Royal after being involved – as Chancellor of the Exchequer – in the financial scandal of the South Sea Bubble. It is one of the great gardens of Europe, contrasting green lawn with stretches of water, both formal and informal. Carefully placed in the landscape are ornamental buildings, from classical temples to Gothic towers. The Aislabie's mansion stood at the north end of the park; it was destroyed by fire in 1945.

The highlight of the southern end of the walk is Markenfield Hall, a rare early 14th-century fortified manor house, built around 1310 for the Markenfield family. You can see the tomb of Sir Thomas Markenfield and his wife Dionisia in Ripon Cathedral. Open on Mondays during the summer, the house still clearly demonstrates how a medieval knight and his family lived; it is part home, part farm. You can still see the chapel and the hall. The gatehouse, convincingly medieval, is actually early 20th century.

Walk 28 Directions

① From the car park turn right uphill, signed 'Harrogate'. At the fork go left, signed 'Markington, Harrogate'. Just after the road bends right, go over a stile beside a gate with bridleway signs.

② Follow the grassy path just inside the ancient Abbey Wall, past a small pond. Go through a waymarked gate and follow the track as it curves round to the right through another gate then left round the farm buildings of Hill House Farm. Go through a small gate near the farmhouse.

③ Turn right then follow the footpath signs to go left at the end of a large shed and then right. Go through a metalled gate on to a track. At the end of the hedge go ahead down the field to a gate into the wood. Follow the track, passing the ruined archway, to descend to a crossroads.

④ Go straight on, signed 'Ripon'. The track climbs to a gate with a Ripon Rowel Walk sign. Follow the track beside the line of trees to a gate on to Whitcliffe Lane. Turn right. At the top of the rise go straight ahead on the metalled road.

WHAT TO LOOK FOR ⓘ
Clearly visible from much of the walk is the spire of St Mary's Church in Studley Park. Now in the care of English Heritage, it was designed for the 1st Marquess of Ripon by the Victorian architect William Burges, between 1871 and 1878, at a cost of £15,000. It was money well spent. Where the exterior is restrained, the interior glows with colour and imagery. A dome over the altar is painted with angels. A carved, winged lion peers from the arches in the chancel. Mosaics show the heavenly city in the flooring. A brass door has a statue of the Virgin and Child. Burges's decoration gets richer from west to east, but throughout the church there is glowing, colourful stained glass. Even the organ seems to be trying to make a statement. In a corner of the south aisle is the alabaster tomb of the Marquess and his wife.

⑤ Go over the cattle grid by Bland Close, then straight ahead with the hedge on your right to reach a stile. Continue along the waymarked track, eventually with woodland to your right. Go over a stile near a metal gate and follow the track as it goes right to reach a gate. Turn right to some farm buildings by Markenfield Hall.

WHILE YOU'RE THERE ⓘ
As well as visiting the abbey and the gardens, take the time to visit nearby Ripon. Its cathedral has a Saxon crypt, and in the stately market place is Britain's oldest free-standing obelisk, designed in 1702 by Hawksmoor. You can discover Ripon's links with Lewis Carroll and how it inspired his Alice books, and see how the law was administered and the wicked punished on the Law and Order Trail.

⑥ Follow the wall to the left, going through a metal gate and straight ahead down the track, through a gate. Follow the track, then a waymark sign, across a field to a stile by a gate. Turn right up the narrow Strait Lane, to emerge into a field.

⑦ Follow the waymarked path beside a field. Go through a gate in the field corner and continue ahead with the hedge to the right. Go through four more gates and follow the track as it curves towards farm buildings. Go over a stile into the farmyard of Morcar Grange, and ahead to the metalled Whitcliffe Lane.

⑧ Turn left and follow the lane as it bends left then right. At the next corner, look for a stile on the right beside a gate. Cross the field half left and go over three stiles, following the waymarked path towards the buildings. Go over a stile and pass between the buildings to reach a metalled road. Turn back to the car park.

WHERE TO EAT AND DRINK ⓘ
The National Trust's visitor centre has a pleasant, airy restaurant offering snacks and meals. There is also a café at the east end of the gardens, near the lake. Nearby Ripon offers a wider choice of pubs, restaurants and tea rooms.

Along the Canal at Gargrave

Following the Leeds and Liverpool Canal from Gargrave.

•DISTANCE•	3½ miles (5.7km)
•MINIMUM TIME•	1hr 30min
•ASCENT / GRADIENT•	114ft (35m)
•LEVEL OF DIFFICULTY•	
•PATHS•	Field paths and tracks, then canal tow path, 4 stiles
•LANDSCAPE•	Farmland and canal side
•SUGGESTED MAP•	aqua3 OS Explorer OL2 Yorkshire Dales – Southern & Western
•START / FINISH•	Grid reference: SD 931539
•DOG FRIENDLINESS•	Dogs should be on leads, except on canal bank
•PARKING•	Opposite church in Gargrave or in village centre
•PUBLIC TOILETS•	By bridge in Gargrave
•CONTRIBUTOR•	David Winpenny

BACKGROUND TO THE WALK

Gargrave has long been a stopping-off point for travellers from the cities of West Yorkshire on their way to the coast at Morecambe or to the Lake District. These days, most of them arrive along the A65 from Skipton, the route formerly taken by horse-drawn coaches. There is still evidence of the village's importance as a coaching centre, especially at the Old Swan Inn. Its position beside the River Aire had also proved important when 18th- and 19th-century surveyors were seeking westward routes for other methods of transport. The walk crosses the railway not long after leaving Gargrave; this is the route that, not far west, becomes the famous Settle-to-Carlisle line. And you will return to the village beside the Leeds and Liverpool Canal.

Earlier Settlers, Mills and Bandages

Although Gargrave is today mostly a 19th-century settlement, there is evidence that the area has been in occupation much longer. The site of a Roman villa has been identified near by, while on West Street, excavation has found the remains of a moated homestead dating from the 13th century, with a smithy and a lime pit, that was reused in the 15th century. By the 18th century there were cotton mills in Gargrave, served by the canal, and weavers were engaged in producing cloth for the clothing industry. Their expertise resulted in the establishment here of one of the village's biggest employers, Johnson & Johnson Medical, where they found workers who could undertake the fine weaving that was needed to produce their bandages.

Canal Digging

In October 1774 the eastern arm of the Leeds and Liverpool canal, snaking its way westwards from Leeds, reached Gargrave. The route, surveyed by John Longbotham and approved by the great canal-builder James Brindley, had been agreed in 1770. Work began at both the Liverpool and the Leeds ends, but there were, inevitably, arguments between the separate committees in Yorkshire and Lancashire about both the route and the finances. It was not until 1810 that the canal had crossed the Pennines, and barges could go from

Leeds to Blackburn, and only in 1816 was the full distance of 127 miles (204km) open to Liverpool. Gargrave benefited not only from the access it gave the village to the raw materials for the cotton mills and the chance to export its cloth, but also as a stopping-place for the bargees.

The walk joins the canal near the lowest of the six locks at Bank Newton, where the canal begins a serpentine course to gain height as it starts its trans-Pennine journey. Near the lock is the former canal company boatyard where boats for maintaining the canal were built. As you walk along the tow path you will cross the Priest Holme Aqueduct, where the canal passes over the River Aire.

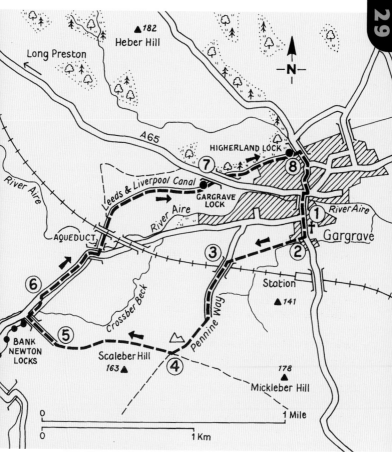

Walk 29 Directions

① Walk along the road with the church tower on your left. Just past **Church Close House** on your right, turn right, following the **Pennine Way** sign. Go over a stone stile in the wall on your left.

② Follow the side of the wall, along the Pennine Way path, which is partly boarded and partly paved here. Go ahead across the field to a waymarked stile, then half left to another stile. Walk towards the top left-hand corner of the field to a stile that leads to Mosber Lane near a railway bridge.

Walk 29

③ Turn left, going over a bridge over the railway, then follow the track through a gateway and climb the hill. After the cattle grid, go half right off the track and across the field to meet another track, which leads to a signpost.

④ At the post, turn right, soon to walk below the wire fence, to reach a waymarked gate in a crossing fence. Go ahead across the field to a pair of gates. Take the waymarked left-hand one and continue ahead, at first with a fence on your right. Follow the track through two gateways into a lane.

WHERE TO EAT AND DRINK ⓘ

Gargrave has several restaurants, tea shops and cafés. The **Dalesman Café** and the **Bridge Restaurant** are both recommended by local people. The **Anchor Inn** beside the canal is a popular dining place for families, and the **Old Swan Inn** on the A65 has meals at lunchtimes and in the evenings.

⑤ Follow the lane between a wall and a fence to descend to the canal by **Bank Newton Locks**. Cross the bridge and turn right along the tow path. The path passes through a gate and goes on to a road.

⑥ Go ahead along the roadside, cross the bridge over the canal then turn left down the winding path

WHILE YOU'RE THERE ⓘ

Explore more canal history at nearby **Skipton**, where the Leeds and Liverpool runs through the heart of the old town. You should also visit the fine parish church at the top of the High Street, and the nearby castle, with its splendid twin-towered gatehouse. Conduit Court, the heart of the castle, has a fine old yew tree in its centre.

under the bridge and continue along the tow path. Pass over a small aqueduct over the river, then under a railway bridge to reach **Gargrave Lock**.

⑦ Beyond the lock, opposite the Anchor Inn, go under the road bridge and continue along the tow path to reach **Bridge 170**, at **Higherland Lock**. Go on to the road by a signpost.

⑧ Turn right down the road, and follow it through the village, past **Gargrave Village Hall**. At the main road turn right, cross the road and go left over the bridge back to the church and the parking place.

WHAT TO LOOK FOR ⓘ

Its worth looking closely at the locks as you walk along the canalside. Bank Newton Locks and the others along this stretch of the canal have the usual paddles, operated by a crank-operated gear, to open the ground holes at the base of the lock gates. At Higherland Lock, however, reached just before you leave the canal, there is a much simpler method. Beside the gates there are apparently two more, rather badly-made, gates. These are the barriers which protect the ground holes, and they are simply pushed aside to let the water through. Look out along the way, too, for the iron markers that detail the distance between Liverpool and Leeds, and the elegant iron signposts. The bridge by which you regain the tow path after a short section along the road is designed to enable the towing horse to change from one side of the canal to the other.

River and Woodland at Bolton Abbey

Over moorland and alongside the Strid to the romantic priory.

•DISTANCE•	6¾ miles (10.9km)
•MINIMUM TIME•	2hrs 30min
•ASCENT / GRADIENT•	870ft (265m) ▲ ▲ ▲
•LEVEL OF DIFFICULTY•	👣 👣 👣
•PATHS•	Field and moorland paths, then riverside paths, 4 stiles
•LANDSCAPE•	Moorland with wide views and riverside woodland
•SUGGESTED MAP•	aqua3 OS Explorer OL2 Yorkshire Dales – Southern & Western
•START / FINISH•	Grid reference: SE 071539
•DOG FRIENDLINESS•	Must be on lead in woodland and on moorland
•PARKING•	Main pay-and-display car park at Bolton Abbey
•PUBLIC TOILETS•	By car park and at Cavendish Pavilion
•CONTRIBUTOR•	David Winpenny

BACKGROUND TO THE WALK

Bolton Abbey has always been one of the showpieces of the Yorkshire Dales, and attracts many visitors, most of whom stay close to the monastic buildings or venture only to the Strid. This walks takes you a little further afield, and has the priory – it was never an abbey – as its climax. After passing under the archway – in fact an aqueduct built in the 18th century to carry water to a mill – you reach Bolton Hall. In part originally the gateway to Bolton Priory, this was later extended as a hunting lodge for the Earls of Cumberland and their successors the Dukes of Devonshire, who still own the estate. The wings are said to be by Sir Joseph Paxton, designer of the Crystal Palace. The walk then passes westwards through woodland to the top of a hill offering excellent views west towards the Aire Valley and north over Barden Fell.

The Thundering Strid

At the entrance to the woodland around the Strid there are information boards that explain the birds and plants you can find here, including the sessile oak. Characteristic of the area, it is distinguished from the pedunculate oak by the fact that its acorns have no stalks. At the Strid itself the River Wharfe thunders through a narrow gorge between rocks. The underlying geology is gritstone, with large white quartz pebbles embedded in it. The Strid was a place loved by the Victorians, but the flow is fast and the river is 30ft (9m) deep here, so don't be tempted to cross; there have been many drownings here over the years. A little further on is the Cavendish Pavilion. A survivor from the early years of the 20th century, the pavilion, called after the family name of the Dukes of Devonshire, has been restored and added to over the years, and is still reminiscent of leisurely sunny days in the 1920s.

The priory was built for Augustinian canons who founded their house here in 1154. The ruins make one of the most romantic scenes in the country, and all the great English artists, from Girtin and Turner on, have painted it. Much of what remains was complete by

1220; the last prior, unaware of the coming storm that would sweep away monastic life, began a tower at the west end. It remained unfinished when the monasteries were suppressed. Most of the buildings fell into ruin, but the nave of the priory church was given to the local people, and it is still their parish church. A former rector, William Carr, spent 54 years here, laying out the paths along the valley that are now enjoyed by so many visitors.

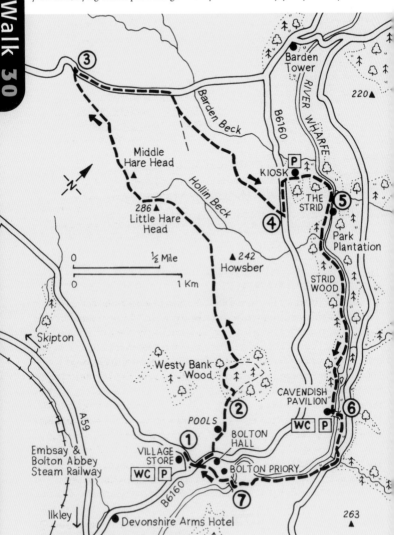

Walk 30 Directions

① Leave car park at its north end, past the **Village Store** and the telephone box. Turn right, walk down the left side of the green, then turn left. Pass under an archway. Opposite the battlemented **Bolton Hall**, turn left on to a track through a signed gate. At the top of the track, go through a gate on the right with a bridleway sign. Walk half left to pass the corner of some pools.

Walk 30

Continue through the gate beyond, and then turn right towards another gate into the wood.

② Go through the gate and follow the signed track through the wood to another gate out into a field. Follow the blue waymarks, many of them painted on rocks, across fields. The path eventually ascends a small hill, with wide views. Descend to a gate, and 20yds (18m) beyond, take a path downhill to the right to a gated stone stile on to the road.

③ Turn right along the road. After 200yds (183m) go right through a gate by a sign 'FP to B6160'. Follow the path across the fields, going over a wooden stile, to reach a wall. Turn right here, following the wall and then some yellow-waymarked posts. Eventually descend to a stone stile on to the road.

④ Turn left and walk along the road for 300yds (274m), then turn right into a car park and pass beside the **Strid Wood Nature Trails Kiosk**. Follow paths, signed 'The Strid', down to the riverbank and turn right to reach the narrowest part of the river at the **Strid**.

⑤ From the Strid, continue on the riverside path until you reach an information board and gateway near the **Cavendish Pavilion**. Go through the gate, turn left by the café and go over the footbridge.

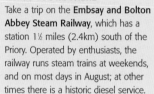

WHILE YOU'RE THERE
Take a trip on the **Embsay and Bolton Abbey Steam Railway**, which has a station 1½ miles (2.4km) south of the Priory. Operated by enthusiasts, the railway runs steam trains at weekends, and on most days in August; at other times there is a historic diesel service.

⑥ Immediately at the end of the bridge turn right signed 'Bolton Abbey'. Follow the path parallel with the river, eventually descending to a bridge beside stepping-stones and the priory.

⑦ Cross the bridge and walk straight ahead up the slope and the steps to a gateway – known as the **Hole in the Wall**. Go through the gateway then straight ahead beside the green to reach the car park.

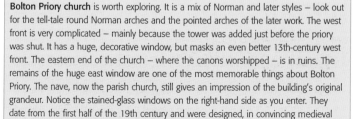

WHAT TO LOOK FOR
Bolton Priory church is worth exploring. It is a mix of Norman and later styles – look out for the tell-tale round Norman arches and the pointed arches of the later work. The west front is very complicated – mainly because the tower was added just before the priory was shut. It has a huge, decorative window, but masks an even better 13th-century west front. The eastern end of the church – where the canons worshipped – is in ruins. The remains of the huge east window are one of the most memorable things about Bolton Priory. The nave, now the parish church, still gives an impression of the building's original grandeur. Notice the stained-glass windows on the right-hand side as you enter. They date from the first half of the 19th century and were designed, in convincing medieval style, by Augustus Pugin, whose decorative work is found in the Houses of Parliament.

Gisburn Forest – a Walk in the Woods

Wooded valleys and heathland – accompanied by the sounds of woodland birds and waterfowl.

·DISTANCE·	3 miles (4.8km)
·MINIMUM TIME·	1hr 30min
·ASCENT / GRADIENT·	285ft (87m) ▲▲▲
·LEVEL OF DIFFICULTY·	🚶 🚶 🚶
·PATHS·	Forest tracks and footpaths
·LANDSCAPE·	Wooded valleys, forest, beckside heathland
·SUGGESTED MAP·	aqua3 OS Explorer OL41 Forest of Bowland & Ribblesdale
·START / FINISH·	Grid reference: SD 732565
·DOG FRIENDLINESS·	Fine for dogs under reasonable control
·PARKING·	Stocks Reservoir car park, Gisburn Forest (free of charge)
·PUBLIC TOILETS·	None on route
·CONTRIBUTOR·	Sheila Bowker

BACKGROUND TO THE WALK

Perfectly placed between the Yorkshire Dales and the Forest of Bowland, Gisburn Forest in the Upper Hodder Valley is the setting for this short, circular stroll. Don't be put off because it's in a forest – it certainly isn't a dire trek through the darkness of a dense conifer plantation. You will walk along open, naturally wooded valleys, beside a tumbling beck and over heathland. You will have views over the reservoir and up to the fells, and you will hear the woodland birdsong and the call of the wildfowl on the water. If you're lucky, you may spot a deer, footprints in the sandy earth confirm their presence.

Stocks Reservoir

The two defining aspects of this walk are the open waters of Stocks Reservoir and the woodlands of Gisburn Forest. The reservoir was built in the 1930s to provide drinking water for the towns of central Lancashire. The village of Stocks was submerged in the process along with many ancient farmsteads. The date stone from one of these can now be seen over the doorway of the post office in Tosside. It was formed by damming the River Hodder and can hold 2.6 billion gallons (12 billion litres) of water when it is at full capacity.

Attractively placed on the edge of the forest, the reservoir is now an important site for wildfowl and 30 different species visit during the average winter period. Amongst the less-commonly sighted of these are red-throated divers, whooper swans, gadwalls and great crested grebes. Amongst the different birds of prey who frequent the area, ospreys and peregrine falcons have been spotted, as well as a rare passing marsh harrier. A birdwatching hide is provided for budding ornithologists, and a pleasant permissive footpath has been constructed around the shoreline.

The Forestry Commission's extensive woodland known as Gisburn Forest was developed at the same time as the reservoir and was opened by HRH Prince George in July 1932. It covers 3,000 acres (1,214ha), making it the largest single forested area in

Lancashire. There are several waymarked trails to be enjoyed, and a cycle network has been developed extending to over 10 miles (16km). Although the majority of the plantations are of the monotonous coniferous variety and are managed principally as a commercial crop, more and more broadleaf trees are being planted to improve the visual aspect and to increase the diversity of wildlife. The forest and the reservoir are now managed in tandem, with inputs from United Utilities, the Forestry Commission and local parishes, to develop a sustainable economic base for this beautiful landscape.

Walk 31

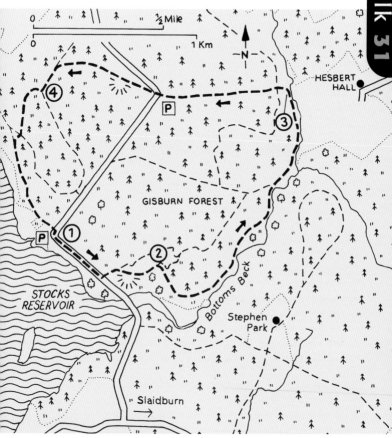

Walk 31 **Directions**

① Leave **Stocks Reservoir car park** in a south easterly direction (straight ahead from the right of the two vehicular entrances). Walk for approximately ¼ mile (400m) then turn left on a forest track marked with a wooden public footpath sign; a red marker post soon confirms your route. There are

good views right, through the trees to the reservoir and causeway with the fells in the background. Keep on the track as it takes you beside open wooded valleys and through natural woodland with a river down on your right.

② Follow the red marker post, set a little off to the right, as it leads you down on to a footpath. The footpath continues with a stream

Walk 31

WHERE TO EAT AND DRINK ⓘ

Nothing is available within the forest itself, so it might be an idea to pack a picnic. Slaidburn, 4½ miles (7.2km) south, has some cafés and the famous 13th-century **Hark to Bounty Inn** which serves good bar meals. **Dunsop Bridge** is a pretty little café stop with the river flowing besides the village green spilling out its flock of mallards on to the grass – especially when the visitors are lunching.

on your left, across a low footbridge to the opposite bank. Soon the tumbling peaty **Bottoms Beck** is on your right with patches of reeds to the left, until a raised embankment leads to higher ground as you pass the farmland of **Hesbert Hall** to the right.

③ Follow the next red marker post as it directs you left to leave the beck, and walk just a few paces to cross straight over a forest track. Follow the path as it takes you gently uphill over boardwalks and heathland, through upright

gateposts by an old broken down wall. Walk straight through **Swinshaw Top** car park to the road and go straight over to take a narrow footpath through the woods by another red marker post. The path opens on to a broadish green swathe but is soon closed in again; however lovely elevated views over the reservoir, left, and the fells ahead make the start of your descent pleasurable.

WHILE YOU'RE THERE ⓘ

The **Forest of Bowland** is a designated Area of Outstanding Natural Beauty (AONB) occupying the north eastern corner of Lancashire. It is a landscape of barren gritstone fells, moorland and steep sided valleys, with 3,260 acres (1,320ha) of open country available to walkers. The village of Dunsop Bridge in the Trough of Bowland claims to be the official centre of the country – a telephone box adjacent to the village green marks the precise spot.

④ Meet a forest track at a bend, proceed straight ahead (slightly right) and follow the track for 200yds (183m) until red posts turn you right, down a footpath with a stream on the right. At a T-junction of footpaths, turn left across open heathland on a clear path back to the car park.

WHAT TO LOOK FOR ⓘ

It's more a case of what to listen for! The **birdsong** throughout the walk, from tiny wrens darting into the bushes in front, to the cry of the curlew skyward is symphonic. Add to that the call of the wildfowl on the reservoir, never far away, and the orchestration is complete.

Tucked Away in Secluded Lothersdale

A short walk with fine views and a glimpse of Lothersdale's industrial past.

•DISTANCE•	4 miles (6.4km)
•MINIMUM TIME•	2hrs
•ASCENT / GRADIENT•	1,509t (100m) ▲▲▲
•LEVEL OF DIFFICULTY•	🚶🚶 🚶🚶 🚶🚶
•PATHS•	Tracks and field paths, some steep sections. 8 stiles
•LANDSCAPE•	Pennine moorland, farmland and industrial relics
•SUGGESTED MAP•	aqua3 OS Explorer OL21 South Pennines
•START / FINISH•	Grid reference: SD 939472
•DOG FRIENDLINESS•	Off lead on final section of walk, from Point ⑤ onwards
•PARKING•	Roadside parking on Carleton to Colne road, north of Clogger Lane
•PUBLIC TOILETS•	None on route
•CONTRIBUTOR•	David Winpenny

BACKGROUND TO THE WALK

Set deep in the rolling countryside to the west of Keighley, Lothersdale is a village of gritstone houses and mill buildings – typical of the small settlements that grew up in the late 18th and early 19th centuries along the river valleys of the West Riding of Yorkshire. The mill dam that you will cross as you enter the village is characteristic of the scale of the industrial enterprise undertaken then – sufficient to employ local people, but too small to fight against the expanding trade of its larger neighbours. Farming and industry had always co-existed here, and today Lothersdale relies on agriculture and tourism – it is a popular stop on the Pennine Way – as well as its role as a base for those who work in the West Yorkshire conurbation.

In the Quarry

The Lothersdale district is of particular interest to geologists. As part of the Ribblesdale Fold Belt, there is a notable anticline at Lothersdale, where the limestone has been tilted by the forces of the earth so that it dips significantly – at angles of anything from 20 to 90 degrees from the horizontal. This dramatic effect is best studied at Raygill Quarry, to the west of the village, where the crest of the anticline is exposed in the rock faces. Between 1876 and 1895 over 35,000 tons of barytes was mined at Raygill. This valuable mineral is a sulphate of barium, which is used in drilling processes, as well as in industrial coatings and linings. The quarrying of the fine carboniferous limestone here continued well into the 20th century, but has now ceased, and the flooded quarry workings have been transformed into a successful trout fishery. Raygill was also the site of a discovery, in 1880, of the bones and teeth of several mammals that died in fissures in the rocks in the period between the ice ages. They included remains of mammoth, rhinoceros, lions, bear, bison and hyena. The bones were taken to Leeds City Museum, where they were damaged by bombing during the Second World War.

Friends and Scholars

The Society of Friends has had a long association with Lothersdale. This once-remote valley provided a haven for Quakers in the persecutions of the 17th century. They built a meeting house here in 1723 and enlarged it in 1799. It had a gallery with unusually designed hatches that could close to create a separate room. The meeting house closed in 1959. In 1800 the Lothersdale Quakers opened one of the earliest Sunday schools anywhere in the world, 'for the preservation of the youth of both sexes, and for their instruction in useful learning.'

Walk 32 **Directions**

① From the car park walk downhill towards the mast on the hillside. Just before the cattle grid turn left up the signed track. At the next signpost turn right, off the track. Follow the wall, then bend left to go over a stile in the wall on your right. Bear left, past a small

plantation, then go diagonally right. Go over a stile and continue downhill with a wall on your right, which bends left to a signed stile on to a metalled drive.

② Turn left along the drive. After the cattle grid bear right along the concrete road and over another cattle grid. Emerge on to a metalled lane and turn left. Follow the lane

WHILE YOU'RE THERE ⓘ
The far-reaching views from the trig point near the end of the walk are matched in splendour by those from the top of **Lund's Tower** near Cowling, 3 miles (4.8km) south east of Lothersdale. Built either to commemorate the Diamond Jubilee of 1897, or the coming of age of Miss Ethel Lund of Malsis Hall down in the valley (or quite possibly both), it shares its ridge with an obelisk, **Wainman's Pinnacle**, while ½ mile (800m) to the south is the 1,000 ton Hitching Stone, said (though who can tell?) to be Yorkshire's largest boulder.

as it bends downwards over a small stream then starts to rise again. Turn right over a cattle grid by the house sign '**The Knott**'.

③ Follow the concrete road, which bends left round the building, then right on to a track. Follow the track with a wall on your left and, at the end, descend towards the pool in the valley. At the bottom of the field go over a stile in the crossing wall, over another stile and across the dam at the end of the small pool and on to the road. Turn left. Just beyond the **Hare and Hounds** pub, turn left at the Pennine Way sign.

④ Follow the track uphill. Leave the track to go right of a large farm building. Follow the wire fence on your right above a wooded valley and continue straight ahead at the top of the valley, now with a stone wall on your left. Pass a broken wall, then take a stile in the wall on your left, signed with an acorn. Go straight across the field to a stone stile on to a lane.

⑤ Cross the lane and continue up the track ahead, signed 'Pennine Way'. Where the concrete farm track bends left, go straight ahead over a stone stile on to a walled track. Follow the wall on your left to a stile, then continue to follow the wall on your left to where it bends sharply left.

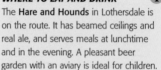

WHERE TO EAT AND DRINK ⓘ
The **Hare and Hounds** in Lothersdale is on the route. It has beamed ceilings and real ale, and serves meals at lunchtime and in the evening. A pleasant beer garden with an aviary is ideal for children.

⑥ Follow the wall left, go over a plank bridge and continue to the trig point on the hilltop. Follow either of the two downhill paths, which converge, and continue past the signpost you passed near the start of the walk. Continue downhill to the road and turn to right to the car parking place.

WHAT TO LOOK FOR ⓘ
Like many places in the area, Lothersdale has close connections with the Brontës – Haworth is less than 8 miles (12.9km) away. At a house called **Stone Gappe** (private) on the hillside ½ mile (800m) east of Lothersdale, Charlotte Brontë was employed as a governess by the Sidgwick family. She had just left her old school, Roe Head, where she had taught for nearly three years. She was not happy in her employment at Stone Gappe, and left after less than three months there. Like many of Charlotte's early experiences, her time at Stone Gappe was used in her novels; the house appears in the first four chapters of *Jane Eyre* as Gateshead Hall, scene of Jane's imprisonment in the Red Room and from where she is taken to Lowood School.

Walk 33

Along the Wharfe to a Victorian Spa Town

From Addingham to Ilkley, along a stretch of the lovely River Wharfe.

•DISTANCE•	5½ miles (8.8km)
•MINIMUM TIME•	2hrs 30min
•ASCENT / GRADIENT•	197ft (60m) ▲▲▲
•LEVEL OF DIFFICULTY•	🚶🚶🚶
•PATHS•	Riverside path and field paths, some road walking, 7 stiles
•LANDSCAPE•	Rolling country and the River Wharfe
•SUGGESTED MAP•	aqua3 OS Explorer 297 Lower Wharfedale
•START / FINISH•	Grid reference: SE 084498
•DOG FRIENDLINESS•	Keep on lead on minor roads
•PARKING•	Lay-by at eastern end of Addingham, on bend where North Street becomes Bark Lane by information panel
•PUBLIC TOILETS•	Ilkley
•CONTRIBUTOR•	John Morrison

BACKGROUND TO THE WALK

Addingham is not one of those compact Yorkshire villages that huddles around a village green. The houses extend for a mile (1.6km) on either side of the main street, with St Peter's Church at the eastern end of the village, close to the river. So it's no surprise that the village used to known as 'Long Addingham', and that it is actually an amalgamation of three separate communities that grew as the textile trades expanded. Having been by-passed in recent years, Addingham is now a quiet backwater.

Within 50 years, from the end of the 17th century, Addingham's population quadrupled, from 500 to 2,000. Even here, at the gateway to the Yorkshire Dales, the textile industries flourished. At the height of the boom, there were six woollen mills in the village. Low Mill, built in 1787, was the scene of a riot by a band of Luddites – weavers and shearers who objected to their jobs being done by machines. Though the mill itself was demolished in 1972, more houses were added to the mill-hands' cottages to create Low Mill Village, a pleasant riverside community.

Ilkley

Visitors from Bath or Cheltenham should feel quite at home in Ilkley, a town that seems to have more in common with Harrogate, its even posher neighbour to the north, than with the textile towns of West Yorkshire. The Romans established an important fort here, believed to be 'Olicana', on a site close to where the parish church is today. Two Roman altars were incorporated into the base of the church tower, and in the churchyard are three Anglo-Saxon crosses from the 9th century. One of the few tangible remains of the Roman settlement is a short stretch of wall near the handsome Manor House, which is now a museum.

Like nearby Harrogate, Ilkley's fortunes changed dramatically with the discovery of medicinal springs. During the reign of Queen Victoria, the great and the good would come here to 'take the waters' and socialise at the town's hydros and hotels. Visitor numbers increased with the coming of the railway, and included such luminaries as Madame Tussaud, George Bernard Shaw and Charles Darwin, taking a well-earned rest after the publication of the *Origin of Species*.

With its open-air swimming pool and riverside promenades, Ilkley was almost an inland resort. Though we have replaced water cures with more sophisticated quackery, Ilkley remains a prosperous town, unashamedly dedicated to the good things of life.

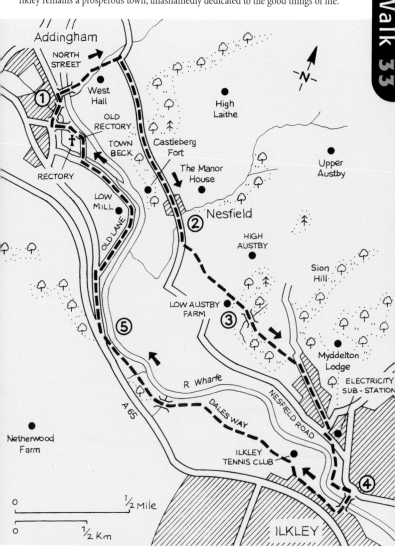

Walk 33 Directions

① Walk 50yds (46m) up the road, and take stone steps down to the right, (signed '**Dales Way**'). Bear immediately right again, and cross the **River Wharfe** on a suspension bridge. Follow a metalled path along a field edge. Cross a stream and join a metalled track between walls that soon emerges at a minor

Walk 33

road by a sharp bend. Go right here; after about ½ mile (800m) of road walking you reach the little community of **Nesfield**.

② About 100yds (91m) beyond the last house, and immediately after the road crosses a stream, bear left up a stony track (signed as a footpath to **High Austby**). Immediately take a stile between two gates. Cross the field ahead, keeping parallel to the road (ignoring a track going left, uphill). There is no obvious path; follow the wall on your right, over a stile. Beyond a small conifer plantation, take a ladder stile in the fence ahead to keep left of **Low Austby Farm**.

③ Cross a footbridge over a stream; beyond a stile you enter woodland. Follow a path downhill, leaving the wood by another step stile. Follow a fence uphill, then cross the middle of a field to locate a stile at the far end, to enter more woodland. Follow an obvious path through the trees, before reaching a road via a wall stile. Go right, downhill, to reach a road junction. Go right again, crossing **Nesfield Road**, and take a path to the left of an electricity sub-station. You have a few minutes of riverside walking before you reach Ilkley's old stone bridge.

④ Cross the bridge. This is your opportunity to explore the spa town of **Ilkley**. Otherwise you should turn right, immediately after the

bridge, on to a riverside path (from here back to **Addingham** you are following the well-signed **Dales Way**). You soon continue along a lane, passing **Ilkley Tennis Club**. Opposite the clubhouse, take a footpath to the left, through a kissing gate, and across pasture. You have seven more kissing gates to negotiate before you are back by the **River Wharfe** again. Cross a stream on a footbridge, and enter woodland. Cross another stream to meet a stony track. Go right, downhill, on this track to the river. Through another kissing gate, you follow a grassy path (with woodland and a fence to your left) before joining the old A65 road. Thanks to the by-pass it is now almost empty of traffic.

⑤ Follow the road by the riverside. After almost ½ mile (800m) of road walking, go right, just before a row of terraced houses, on to **Old Lane**. Pass between the houses of a new development – **Low Mill Village** – to locate a riverside path, now metalled, at the far side. Once you have passed the Rectory on the left, and the grounds of the **Old Rectory** on your right, look for a kissing gate on the right. Take steps and follow the path to a tiny arched bridge over **Town Beck**. You have a grassy path across pasture, in front of the church, before taking another bridge, between houses, to re-emerge on **North Street** in **Addingham**.

Ilkley Moor and the Twelve Apostles

Standing stones and a brief look at some intriguing historic features.

•DISTANCE•	4½ miles (7.2km)
•MINIMUM TIME•	2hrs 30min
•ASCENT / GRADIENT•	425ft (130m) ▲▲▲
•LEVEL OF DIFFICULTY•	🚶 🚶 🚶
•PATHS•	Good moorland paths, some steep paths towards end of walk
•LANDSCAPE•	Mostly open heather moorland, and gritstone crags
•SUGGESTED MAP•	aqua3 OS Explorer 297 Lower Wharfedale
•START / FINISH•	Grid reference: SE 132467
•DOG FRIENDLINESS•	Under control where sheep graze freely on moorland
•PARKING•	Off-road parking on Hangingstone Road, opposite Cow and Calf rocks, also a pay-and-display car park
•PUBLIC TOILETS•	In pay-and-display car park near Cow and Calf rocks
•CONTRIBUTOR•	John Morrison

BACKGROUND TO THE WALK

Ilkley Moor is a long ridge of millstone grit, immediately to the south of Ilkley. With or without a hat, Ilkley Moor is a special place... not just for walkers, but for lovers of archaeological relics too. These extensive heather moors are identified on maps as Rombalds Moor, named after a legendary giant who roamed the area. But, thanks to the famous song – Yorkshire's unofficial anthem – Ilkley Moor is how it's always known.

An Ancient Ring

The Twelve Apostles is a ring of Bronze-Age standing stones sited close to the meeting of two ancient routes across the moor. If you expect to find something of Stonehenge proportions, you will be disappointed. The twelve slabs of millstone grit (there were more stones originally, probably twenty, with one at the centre) are arranged in a circle approximately 50ft (15m) in diameter. The tallest of the stones is little more than 3ft (1m). The circle is, nevertheless, a genuinely ancient monument.

The Twelve Apostles are merely the most visible evidence of 7,000 years of occupation of these moors. There are other, smaller circles too, and Ilkley Moor is celebrated for its Bronze-Age rock carvings, many showing the familiar 'cup and ring' designs. The most famous of these rocks features a sinuous swastika: traditionally a symbol of good luck, until the Nazis corrupted it. There are milestones, dating from more recent times, which would have given comfort and guidance to travellers across these lonely moors. In addition to Pancake and Haystack rocks, seen on this walk, there are dozens of other natural gritstone rock formations. The biggest and best known are the Cow and Calf, close to the start of this walk, where climbers practise their holds and rope work.

A guidebook of 1829 described Ilkley as a little village. It was the discovery of mineral springs that transformed Ilkley into a prosperous spa town. Dr William Mcleod arrived here

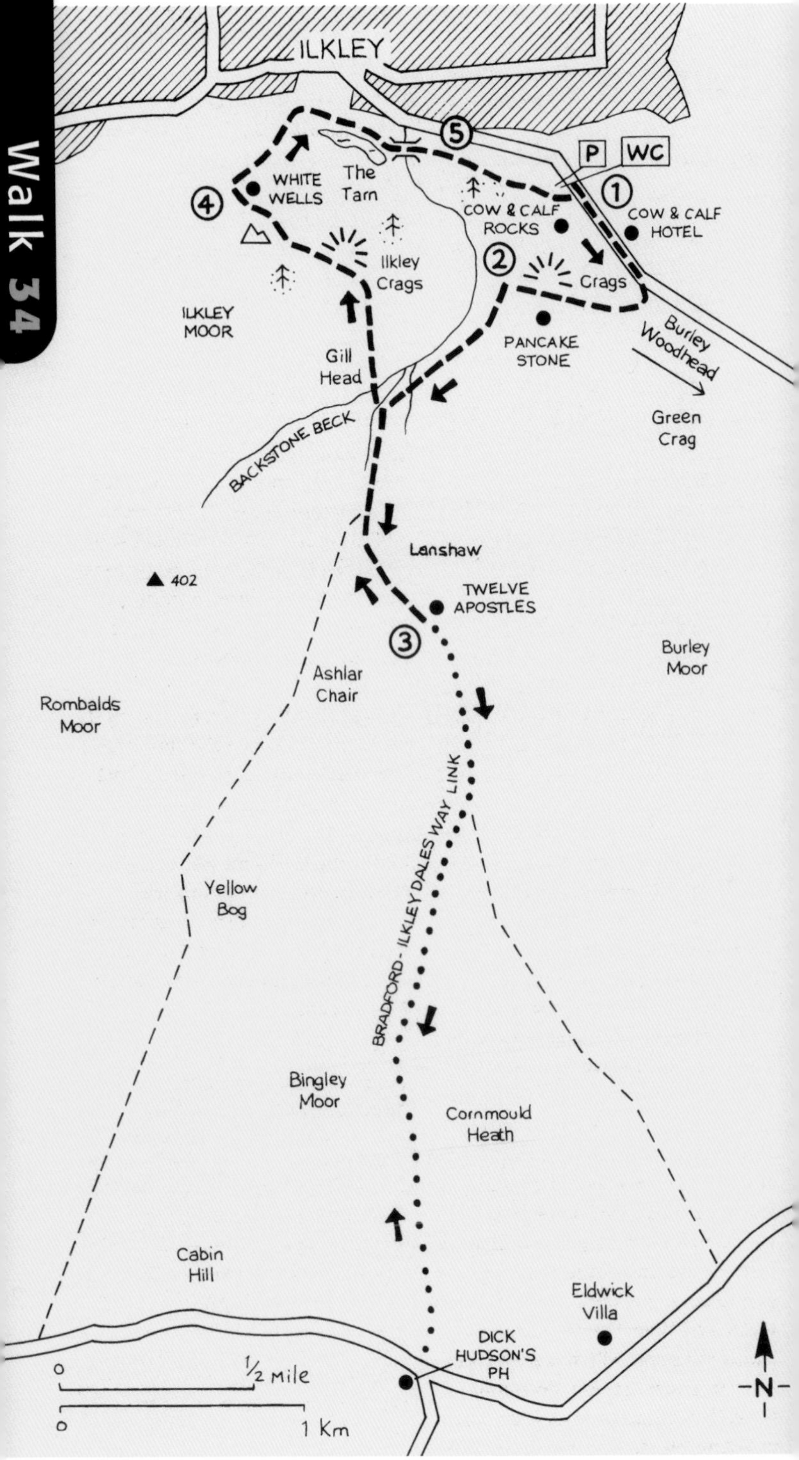

ILKLEY

⑤

④ WHITE WELLS
The Tarn

COW & CALF ROCKS

P WC

① COW & CALF HOTEL

② Crags

Ilkley Crags

ILKLEY MOOR

Gill Head

PANCAKE STONE

Burley Woodhead

Green Crag

BACKSTONE BECK

Lanshaw

▲ 402

TWELVE APOSTLES

③

Ashlar Chair

Burley Moor

Rombalds Moor

Yellow Bog

BRADFORD - ILKLEY DALES WAY LINK

Bingley Moor

Cornmould Heath

Cabin Hill

Eldwick Villa

½ mile

DICK HUDSON'S PH

1 Km

-N-

Walk 34

in 1847, recognised the town's potential and spent the next 25 years creating a place where well-heeled hypochondriacs could 'take the waters' in upmarket surroundings.

Dr Mcleod recognised – or perhaps just imagined – the curative properties of cold water. He vigorously promoted what he called the 'Ilkley Cure', a strict regime of exercise and cold baths. Luxurious hotels known as 'hydros', precursors of today's health farms, sprang up around the town to cater for the influx of visitors.

Predating the town's popularity as a spa is White Wells, built in 1700 around one of the original springs. A century later a pair of plunge baths were added, where visitors and locals alike could enjoy the masochistic pleasures of bathing in cold water. Enjoying extensive views over the town, the building is still painted white. White Wells is now a visitor centre that's open to (non-bathing) visitors at weekends.

Walk 34 Directions

① Walk up the road; 150yds (138m) beyond the **Cow and Calf Hotel**, where the road bears left, fork right up a grassy path. Scramble up the ridge to the **Pancake Stone**. Bear right on a path along the edge of the ridge, cross a stony track and pass the **Haystack Rock**. From here your track slowly wheels left, to run parallel to **Backstone Beck**, uphill, on to open heather moorland.

② At the top you meet the **Bradford–Ilkley Dales Way** link path. Go left here; soon you are walking on a section of duckboarding. Pass a boundary stone at the top of the next rise, and continue to the ring of stones known as the **Twelve Apostles**.

③ Retrace your steps from the **Twelve Apostles**, and continue along the **Dales Way** link path. Having crossed **Backstone Beck**, you soon leave the open moorland behind, and find yourself on top of a ridge. Enjoy the views across **Ilkley** and **Wharfedale**, before taking the path (which is stepped in some in places) steeply downhill. Beneath a clump of trees you come to **White Wells**.

④ Bear right, passing to the left of ponds, on a path, downhill. Aim for a pyramid-shaped rock, after which you emerge on to a metalled track. Walk either way around the tarn. At the far end take a path, uphill at first, then down to cross **Backstone Beck** again on a little footbridge, then one last haul uphill to reach the **Cow and Calf** rocks.

⑤ Take a few minutes to investigate the rocks and watch the climbers. From here a paved path leads back to the car park.

Extending the Walk

A classic extension of this walk takes you across the moor from the **Twelve Apostles** (Point ③) to the pub at **Dick Hudson's**, returning by the same route.

WHERE TO EAT AND DRINK   ⓘ

This classic walk across Ilkley Moor almost demands that you follow in the footsteps of generations of walkers, by calling in at **Dick Hudson's** for a hearty meal. The **Cow and Calf Hotel**, at the start of the walk, near the famous rocks, is another option for refreshments. If you've time to wander around Ilkley itself, the first hostelry you'll come to is the **Midland Hotel**, serving bar meals and real ales. Further along the street, on The Grove, you'll find a branch of the famous **Betty's Tea Rooms**.

In Giant Rombald's Footsteps

A taste of West Yorkshire moorland from the village of Burley in Wharfedale.

•DISTANCE•	4 miles (6.4km)
•MINIMUM TIME•	2hrs
•ASCENT / GRADIENT•	560ft (170m) ▲▲▲
•LEVEL OF DIFFICULTY•	🚶 🚶 🚶
•PATHS•	Good tracks and moorland paths, 5 stiles
•LANDSCAPE•	Moor and arable land
•SUGGESTED MAP•	aqua3 OS Explorer 297 Lower Wharfedale
•START / FINISH•	Grid reference: SE 163457
•DOG FRIENDLINESS•	Can be off lead but watch for grazing sheep
•PARKING•	Burley in Wharfedale Station car park
•PUBLIC TOILETS•	At railway station
•CONTRIBUTOR•	John Morrison

BACKGROUND TO THE WALK

According to the legend, a giant by the name of Rombald used to live in these parts. While striding across the moor that now bears his name (in some versions of the story he was being chased by his angry wife) he dislodged a stone from a gritstone outcrop, and thus created the Calf, of the Cow and Calf rocks. Giants such as Rombald and Wade – and even the Devil himself – were apparently busy all over Yorkshire, dropping stones or creating big holes in the ground. It was perhaps an appealing way of accounting for some of the more unusual features of the landscape. Rombalds Moor is pitted with old quarries, from which good quality stone was won. The Cow and Calf rocks used to be a complete family unit, but the rock known as the Bull was broken up to provide building stone.

The Hermit of Rombalds Moor

At Burley Woodhead a public house called the Hermit commemorates Job Senior, a local character with a chequered career. Job worked as a farm labourer, before succumbing to the demon drink. He met an elderly widow of independent means, who lived in a cottage at Coldstream Beck, on the edge of Rombalds Moor. Thinking he might get his hands on her money and home, Job married the old crone. Though she died soon after, Job took no profit. The family of her first husband pulled the cottage down, in Job's absence, leaving him homeless and penniless once more.

Enraged, he built himself a tiny hovel from the ruins of the house. Here he lived in filth and squalor on a diet of home-grown potatoes, which he roasted on a peat fire. He cut a strange figure, with a coat of multi-coloured patches and trousers held up with twine. He had long, lank hair, a matted beard and his legs were bandaged with straw. He made slow, rheumatic progress around Rombalds Moor with the aid of two crooked sticks.

His eccentric lifestyle soon had people flocking to see him. He offered weather predictions, and even advised visitors about their love lives. The possessor of a remarkable voice, he 'sang for his supper' as he lay on his bed of dried bracken and heather. These impromptu performances encouraged Job to sing in nearby villages, and even in the theatres of Leeds and Bradford. His speciality was sacred songs, which he would deliver with great feeling. Nevertheless, his unwashed appearance meant that accommodation was never forthcoming, forcing him to bed down in barns or outhouses. It was while staying in a barn that he was struck down with cholera. He was taken to Carlton Workhouse, where he died in 1857, aged 77. A huge crowd of people gathered at his funeral. Job Senior, the hermit of Rombalds Moor, was buried in the churchyard of Burley in Wharfedale. He's commemorated in the old sign hanging over the entrance at the Hermit pub.

Walk 35 Directions

① From the station car park, cross the line via a footbridge and go left along a quiet lane. Follow the lane past houses and between fields up to **Hag Farm**.

② When the track wheels right, into the farmyard, keep left on a track to a stile and a gate.

Accompany a wall downhill; after 100yds (91m) take a gap stile in the wall. Bear off sharply to the right, to follow a stream up to another wall and gap stile. Follow a fence uphill to take another stile, cross the stream on a footbridge and join the approach road to a group of houses. Walk uphill to meet the **Guiseley–Ilkley road**. (To visit the **Hermit** pub you would need to go right here, for ¼ mile/400m.)

Walk 35

Cross the road and continue on a stony track ahead. After just 50yds (46m), ford a stream and follow a path uphill through woodland, on to a path hemmed in by hedges. Out on to open pasture you come to a gate. Follow the wall to your right, soon leaving it to take an indistinct path uphill.

③ Meet a stony track and follow it to the right, along the moorland edge. Follow a wall to a stile by a gate. Immediately after, keep right when the track forks. Keep right again as you approach a small brick building. Route-finding is now easy, as the track wheels around a farm. Keep left at the next farm (called **York View** because, on a clear day, you can see York Minster from here) to make a slow descent, following a wall on your right. As you approach a third farm, look out for two barns and a gate, on the right. Take an indistinct path to the

left here, passing a small quarry. Enjoy level walking through bracken with great views over **Lower Wharfedale**. Go steeply down a little ravine and cross a beck; continue up the other side. Before you reach the top, bear right and follow a path downhill to meet a road by a sharp bend.

④ Walk 100yds (91m) down the road, to another sharp right-hand bend. Bear left here (signed '**Ilkley Moor Garden Centre**'). Keep left of the garden centre itself, by continuing down the stony track. Keep left of a house, the **Lodge**; when the track bears sharp left towards a farm, your route is to the right, through a kissing gate, to follow a field path downhill with woodland to the left. After another kissing gate, follow a fence – then a wall – on the right. Beyond a third kissing gate and another gate, you join a tree-lined track heading to the right.

⑤ Meet a road and walk downhill back to the railway station car park.

Golden Acre and Breary Marsh

A walk of great variety in the rolling countryside to the north of Leeds.

•DISTANCE•	5 miles (8km)
•MINIMUM TIME•	2hrs 30min
•ASCENT / GRADIENT•	100ft (30m)
•LEVEL OF DIFFICULTY•	
•PATHS•	Good paths, tracks and quiet roads, 21 stiles
•LANDSCAPE•	Parkland, woods and arable country
•SUGGESTED MAP•	aqua3 OS Explorer 297 Lower Wharfedale
•START / FINISH•	Grid reference: SE 266418
•DOG FRIENDLINESS•	On lead when in park, due to wildfowl
•PARKING•	Golden Acre Park car park, across road from park itself, on A660 just south of Bramhope
•PUBLIC TOILETS•	Golden Acre Park, at start of walk
•CONTRIBUTOR•	John Morrison

BACKGROUND TO THE WALK

Leeds is fortunate to have so many green spaces. Some, like Roundhay Park, are long established; others, like the Kirkstall Valley nature reserve, have been created from post-industrial wasteland. But none have had a more chequered history than Golden Acre Park, 6 miles (9.7km) north of the city on the main A660.

Amusement Park

The park originally opened in 1932 as an amusement park. The attractions included a miniature railway, nearly 2 miles (3.2km) in length, complete with dining car. The lake was the centre of much activity, with motor launches, dinghies for hire and races by the Yorkshire Hydroplane Racing Squadron. An open-air lido known, somewhat exotically, as the Blue Lagoon, offered unheated swimming and the prospect of goose-pimples. The Winter Gardens Dance Hall boasted that it had 'the largest dance floor in Yorkshire'.

Though visitors initially flocked to Golden Acre Park, the novelty soon wore off. By the end of the 1938 season the amusement park had closed down and was sold to Leeds City Council. The site was subsequently transformed into botanical gardens – a process that's continued ever since. The hillside overlooking the lake has been lovingly planted with trees and unusual plants, including rock gardens and fine displays of rhododendrons.

The boats are long gone; the lake is now a haven for wildfowl. Within these 127 acres (51ha) – the 'Golden Acre' name was as fanciful as 'the Blue Lagoon' – is a wide variety of wildlife habitats, from open heathland to an old quarry. Lovers of birds, trees and flowers will find plenty to interest them at every season of the year. One of the few echoes of the original Golden Acre Park is a café situated close to the entrance. Reflecting the park's increasing popularity, a large car park has been built on the opposite side of the main road, with pedestrian access to the park via a tunnel beneath the road. This intriguing park offers excellent walking, and wheelchair users, too, can make a circuit of the lake on a broad path.

Walk 36

Walk 36 **Directions**

① From the far left end of the car park, take steps and an underpass beneath the road, into **Golden Acre Park**. Take one of the paths to the left or the right around the lake; at the far left end of the lake leave the park by a gate (signed '**Meanwood Valley Trail**'). Bear left, along a tree-lined path, to a T-junction of roads. Take the road ahead, up to the aptly-named **Five Lane Ends**.

② Take the second road on the left (**Eccup Moor Road**), passing a dog training centre on the left and a golf course on the right. Ignore side turnings till you reach the outbuildings of **Bank House Farm**, where you take a farm track to the left. It soon narrows to become a path between hedgerows. About 50yds (46m) before the footpath bears right take a stile in the fence on your left, to join a field path to a wall stile. Cross another field to meet a road (the **New Inn** is just along the road to your right).

WHERE TO EAT AND DRINK
It requires the shortest of detours, at about the half-way point of this walk, to visit the **New Inn**, near Eccup. A sign welcomes walkers – as do the open fires and beer garden – and an extensive menu will whet your appetite.

cross a field to the bottom right-hand corner and another stile. Head left, across the next field, to a stile, that brings you out at the A660 by a roundabout.

⑤ Cross the main road and take **The Sycamores** ahead. After 250yds (230m) take a waymarked stile on the left to join a field-edge footpath with a hedge on the left. Cross a succession of five stiles, and then tiny Marsh Beck, before skirting an area of woodland on your right. Beyond a ladder stile you join a farm track, bearing left past a farmhouse to enter **Fish Pond Plantation** via a gate.

WHAT TO LOOK FOR
Look for the damp-loving alder trees in Breary Marsh. Their seeds are designed to float on the water. During winter you should see little siskins (a type of finch) feeding on the seeds, of which they are particularly fond. You may also spy the vivid caterpillar of the alder moth.

③ Go left along the road for just 20yds (18m) to take a stile on your right (signposted '**Dales Way**'), leading to a field path. After another stile you join a track ahead over a further stile and uphill with a wall to your left. Veer right across pasture to a wall stile and continue towards **Lineham Farm**. Beyond two more wall stiles you pass the farm buildings and join a good track. When the track goes left you keep straight ahead on a path between fences. After field-edge walking, and a further three stiles, you reach a road.

④ Go right along the road for 150yds (138m) and take a waymarked stile on the left by a gate. Follow the field-edge path with a fence on your left. Through two kissing gates bear left across a field, keeping to the right of **Breary Grange Farm**. After a ladder stile,

⑥ Bear right, through the wood, soon reaching the retaining wall of a small stretch of water known locally as **Paul's Pond**. Bear left here on a woodland path accompanying a stream. Having crossed the stream on a footbridge, you soon join a duckboarded walkway that keeps you dry-footed as you cross **Breary Marsh**. The walkway meanders back towards the underpass beneath the A660 road. Go left, in front of it, back into the car park.

WHILE YOU'RE THERE
Take a look at Bramhope's **Puritan Chapel**, adjacent to the entrance to the Post House Hotel on the A660, as it passes through the village. This small, simple chapel was built in 1649, by devout Puritan Robert Dyneley. It contains original furnishings, including box pews and a three-deck pulpit.

Harewood's Treasure House

A stately home with parkland by 'Capability' Brown, a few miles from Leeds.

•DISTANCE•	6½ miles (10.4km)
•MINIMUM TIME•	3hrs
•ASCENT / GRADIENT•	164ft (50m) ▲▲▲
•LEVEL OF DIFFICULTY•	🚶🚶 🚶🚶 🚶🚶
•PATHS•	Good paths and parkland tracks all the way, 2 stiles
•LANDSCAPE•	Arable and parkland
•SUGGESTED MAP•	aqua3 OS Explorer 289 Leeds
•START / FINISH•	Grid reference: SE 332450
•DOG FRIENDLINESS•	Keep under control through estate and on A658
•PARKING•	Limited in Harewood village. From traffic lights, take A658, and park in first lay-by on left
•PUBLIC TOILETS•	None on route; in Harewood House if you pay to go in
•CONTRIBUTOR•	John Morrison

BACKGROUND TO THE WALK

The grand old houses of West Yorkshire tend to be in the form of 'Halifax' houses (such as East Riddlesden Hall. Self-made yeomen and merchant clothiers built their mansions to show the world that they'd made their 'brass'. But Harewood House, on the edge of Leeds, is more ambitious, and is still one of the great treasure houses of England.

Vision into Reality

The Harewood Estate passed through a number of wealthy hands during the 16th and 17th centuries, eventually being bought by the Lascelles family who still own the house today. Edwin Lascelles left the 12th-century castle in its ruinous state, to overlook the broad valley of the River Wharfe, but demolished the old hall. He wanted to create something very special in its place and hired the best architects and designers to turn his vision into reality.

John Carr of York created a veritable palace of a house, in an imposing neo-classical style and laid out the estate village of Harewood too. The interior of the building was designed by Robert Adam, now best remembered for his fireplaces. Thomas Chippendale, born in nearby Otley, made furniture for every room, as part of the house's original plans. The foundations were laid in 1759; 12 years later the house was finished. Inside the house are paintings by J M W Turner and Thomas Girtin, who both stayed and painted at the house. Turner was particularly taken with the area, producing pictures of many local landmarks. The sumptuous interior, full of family portraits, ornate plasterwork and silk hangings, is in sharp contrast to life below stairs, in the kitchen and scullery.

The house sits in extensive grounds, which were preened and groomed to be every bit as magnificent as the house. They were shaped by Lancelot 'Capability' Brown, the most renowned designer of the English landscape. In addition to the formal gardens, he created the lake and the woodland paths you will take on this walk. Like so many of England's stateliest homes, Harewood House has had to earn its keep in recent years. The bird garden was the first commercial venture, but now the house hosts events such as art exhibitions, vintage car rallies and even open-air concerts.

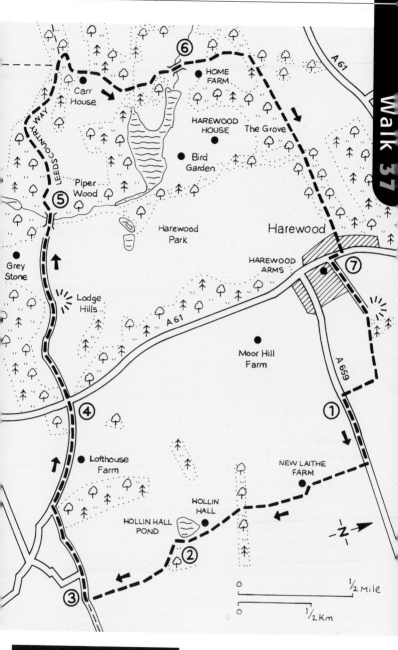

Walk 37

Walk 37 Directions

① From the lay-by walk 50yds (46m) away from the village of **Harewood**, cross the road and walk right, down the access track to

New Laithe Farm. Keep to the left of the farm buildings, on a grassy track heading into the valley bottom. Go through two gates and bear half left up a field, towards **Hollin Hall**. Keep left of the buildings to pass **Hollin Hall Pond**.

Walk 37

② Beyond the pond take a gate and follow a track to the left, uphill, skirting woodland. Continue uphill on a field-edge path with a hedgerow to your left. Pass through two gates, the path now being enclosed between hedges.

③ Bear right at the top of the hill to have easy, level walking on an enclosed sandy track (you are now joining the **Leeds Country Way**). Keep straight ahead when the track forks, through a gate. Skirt woodland to emerge at a road; bear right here to arrive at the main A61.

WHILE YOU'RE THERE ℹ

While the walk described here uses rights of way through the grounds of **Harewood House**, you need to pay if you want to investigate the house itself, or the bird gardens, or the many other attractions. Make a day of it: do the walk in the morning, have lunch at the Harewood Arms and investigate the unrivalled splendour of Harewood House in the afternoon.

---

④ Cross the road to enter the **Harewood Estate** (via the right-hand gate, between imposing gate-posts). Follow the broad track ahead, through landscaped parkland, soon getting views of **Harewood House** to the right. Enter woodland through a gate, bearing immediately left after a stone bridge.

⑤ Bear right after 100yds (91m), as the track forks. At a crossing of tracks, bear right, downhill, still through woodland. At the next two forks keep first right, then left, to pass a farm. Follow a good track down towards the lake. Go through a gate, keep left of a high brick wall and walk uphill to join a metalled access road to the left.

WHERE TO EAT AND DRINK ℹ

Apart from designing the house itself, John Carr was also responsible for the estate village of Harewood. The neat terraced houses, though modest by comparison, have architectural echoes of the big house. Almost opposite the main gates of Harewood House is the **Harewood Arms**, a former coaching inn that offers the chance of a drink or meal towards the end of the walk. If the weather is kind, you can rest your legs in the beer garden.

Walk down past a house and keep straight ahead at crossroads. Cross a bridge and follow the lane up to a gate, soon passing **Home Farm** (now converted to business units).

⑥ Follow the road through pastureland, keeping right, uphill, at a choice of routes. Continue through woodland until you come to the few houses that comprise the estate village of **Harewood**.

⑦ Cross the main A61 road and walk right, for just 50yds (46m), to take a metalled drive immediately before the **Harewood Arms**. Pass **Maltkiln House**, keeping straight on, through a gate, as the road becomes a track. Enjoy great views over **Lower Wharfedale**. After a stile by a gate, take another stile in the fence to your right and follow a field path back to the A659 road and your car.

WHAT TO LOOK FOR ℹ

The **red kite**, a beautiful fork-tailed bird of prey, used to be a familiar sight. But the numbers had dwindled to just a few pairs, mostly in Wales, due to centuries of persecution. There is now a new initiative to reintroduce the red kite to Yorkshire, and a number of birds have been released at Harewood House. You may be lucky enough to spot one.

Wetherby and the River Wharfe

Around a handsome country market town and along a stretch of the mature River Wharfe.

•DISTANCE•	3½ miles (5.7km)
•MINIMUM TIME•	2hrs
•ASCENT / GRADIENT•	65ft (20m) ▲ ▲ ▲
•LEVEL OF DIFFICULTY•	🚶 🚶 🚶
•PATHS•	Field paths and good tracks, a little road walking, 1 stile
•LANDSCAPE•	Arable land, mostly on flat
•SUGGESTED MAP•	aqua3 OS Explorer 289 Leeds
•START / FINISH•	Grid reference: SE 405479
•DOG FRIENDLINESS•	No particular problems
•PARKING•	Free car parking in Wilderness car park, close to river, just over bridge as you drive into Wetherby from south
•PUBLIC TOILETS•	Wetherby
•CONTRIBUTOR•	John Morrison

BACKGROUND TO THE WALK

Wetherby, at the north east corner of the county, is not your typical West Yorkshire town. Most of the houses are built of pale stone, topped with roofs of red tiles – a type of architecture more usually found in North Yorkshire. With its riverside developments and air of prosperity, the Wetherby of today is a favoured place to live. The flat, arable landscape, too, is very different to Pennine Yorkshire. Here, on the fringes of the Vale of York, the soil is rich and dark and productive – the fields divided up by fences and hedgerows rather than dry-stone walls.

Historic Town

The town has a long history. A brief glance at an Ordnance Survey map reveals that Wetherby grew up around a tight curve in the River Wharfe. Its importance as a river crossing was recognised by the building of a castle, possibly in the 12th century, of which only the foundations remain. The first mention of a bridge was in 1233. A few years later, in 1240, the Knights Templar were granted a royal charter to hold a market in Wetherby.

At Flint Mill, visited on this walk, flints were ground for use in the pottery industry of Leeds. The town also had two corn mills, powered by water from the River Wharfe. The distinctive weir helped to maintain a good head of water to turn the waterwheels. In general though, the Industrial Revolution made very little impression on Wetherby.

The town grew in importance not from what it made, but from where it was situated. In the days of coach travel, the 400-mile (648km) trip between London and Edinburgh was quite an ordeal for passengers and horses alike. And Wetherby, at the half-way point of the journey, became a convenient stop for mail and passenger coaches. The trade was busiest during the second half of the 18th century, when the town had upwards of 40 inns and alehouses. Coaching inns such as the Swan, the Talbot and the Angel catered for weary travellers and provided stabling for the horses. The Angel was known as 'the Halfway House' and had stables for more than a hundred horses. The Great North Road ran across the town's splendid arched bridge, and right through the middle of the town. With coaches arriving and departing daily, it must have presented a busy scene

When the railway arrived in the 1840s, Wetherby's role as a staging post went into decline. The Great North Road was eventually re-routed – to skirt around the town, rather than run straight through the centre. Even the name was lost, with the road now being known, more prosaically, as the A1. When Dr Beeching wielded his axe in 1964, Wetherby lost its railway too. Ironically, a town that had once been synonymous with coach travel is now a peaceful backwater, re-inventing itself once again as an upmarket commuter town. The area around the River Wharfe is being renovated, to provide riverside apartments, pleasant walks and picnic sites. These days most people will probably know the town from listening to the racing results.

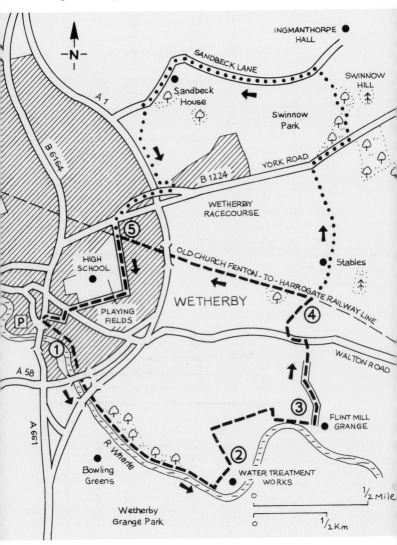

Walk 38 Directions

① Walk to the far end of the car park, to follow a path with the **River Wharfe** on the right and cliffs to the left. You pass in quick succession beneath the shallow arches of two modern bridges, carrying the A58 and A1 roads across the **Wharfe**. Go through a kissing gate to continue on a riverside path, soon with open fields on your left. Take another kissing gate to arrive at Wetherby's **water treatment works**.

② Go left here, up a track around the perimeter fence. After 150yds (138m) you meet a metalled track at the works' main entrance; go left here. At the top of an incline, where the track bears slightly to the right, you have a choice of routes. Your path is sharp right, along a grassy track between fields. You soon approach the wooded slope that overlooks the **River Wharfe**. Take a stile, and follow the line of trees to a farm, **Flint Mill Grange**. Enter the farmyard and take the farm access road to the left.

③ Meet **Walton Road** and walk left for 75yds (68m); then go right,

along a metalled drive (this is signed as both a bridleway and the entrance to **Wetherby Racecourse**). After a gate you have a choice of routes, bear left here, downhill, to join the trackbed of the old Church Fenton-to-Harrogate railway line.

④ Go left, to enjoy level walking along the railway trackbed, until you approach the A1 road, raised up on an embankment as it skirts around Wetherby. Take the underpass beneath the road, and bear right along **Freemans Way**, until you meet **Hallfield Lane**.

⑤ Walk left, along **Hallfield Lane**, which bears right around the playing fields of **Wetherby High School** and back into the centre of **Wetherby**.

Extending the Walk

You can see more of the famous **Wetherby Racecourse** by crossing the old railway at Point ④ and following tracks around to **Sandbeck Lane**, returning to the main walk at Point ⑤.

Walk 39

To Pendle with Witches and Water

Up Ogden's reservoirs to the inspiring viewpoint atop Pendle Hill to discover witchcraft and folklore.

•DISTANCE•	4½ miles (7.2km)
•MINIMUM TIME•	2hrs 30min
•ASCENT / GRADIENT•	1,095ft (334m) ▲▲▲
•LEVEL OF DIFFICULTY•	🚶🚶🚶
•PATHS•	Defined paths, lots of kissing gates but virtually no stiles
•LANDSCAPE•	Wooded valleys, moorland, hilltop views
•SUGGESTED MAP•	aqua3 OS Explorer OL41 Forest of Bowland & Ribblesdale
•START / FINISH•	Grid reference: SD 823403
•DOG FRIENDLINESS•	Virtually no stiles, on lead near livestock on moorland
•PARKING•	Car park in Barley – free of charge (voluntary contributions)
•PUBLIC TOILETS•	At car park
•CONTRIBUTOR•	Sheila Bowker

BACKGROUND TO THE WALK

This walk commences in the commendable village of Barley, which, in 1324, was known as Barelegh – an infertile lea or meadow. It follows much of the route of the Pendle Way signposted by a black witch flying on her broomstick across a yellow sky. You climb gently past the Lower Ogden Reservoir and the Upper Ogden Reservoir to the steep sided Ogden Clough, then strike off up Boar Clough where the vegetation is indicative of acidic peat: ferns uncurl above bilberry shrubs and verdant patches of moss and white bog cotton complete the patchwork. The going is soft on the peaty ground across Barley Moor to the summit of Pendle Hill, and such is the spellbinding spirit of the area that dark figures on the skyline above could easily be mistaken for witches! The descent down the Big End is steep but quick, followed by a lovely tree-lined walk beside a tiny beck to return to Barley.

Referred to as a sleeping lion, Pendle Hill slopes gently up the lion's back to fall away sharply down the face, known as the Big End. The summit affords a spectacular birds-eye view over the Ribble Valley to Yorkshire's Three Peaks in the north and Lancashire's cotton towns of Padiham and Burnley nestling beneath the Pennine hills to the south. At 1,827ft (557m) the hill is constructed of gritstone and limestone, a combination that strongly influences the contrasting Pendle scenery. On the summit is the Beacon, a Bronze-Age burial mound thought to be possibly 7,000 years old. It was Pendle Hill that George Fox climbed in 1652 and where he had his vision of enlightenment that led to him founding the Quaker movement. 'I was moved of the Lord to go up the top of it, which I did with much ado, as it was so very steep and high.'

Pendle Witches

Witch comes from the Anglo-Saxon word wicca, meaning 'the wise ones' who thought they possessed magical powers that could be put to use at times of pagan ritual. The Demdikes of Malkin Tower and the Chattox's of Higham were matriarchal families who terrorised the

Pendle area in the early 17th century. These self-confessed witches were accused of cursing cattle and turning them into cats, turning the ale in the inn at Higham sour and bewitching the landlord's son to death, and paralysing a pedlar on the road to Colne. These were difficult times for independent women, witches or not and some 19 Pendle residents were eventually taken to the gaol at Lancaster Castle where they were charged with witchcraft. The Witch Trial took place in August 1612 and, after some dubious confessions, resulted in the execution by hanging of nine Pendle women.

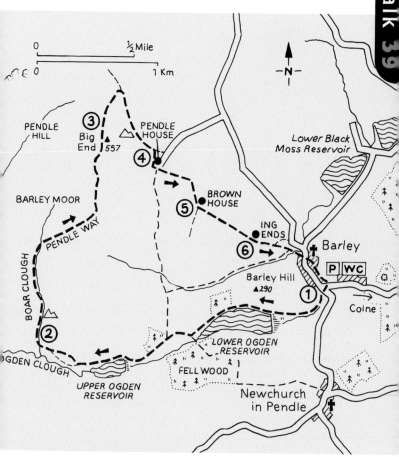

Walk 39 **Directions**

① Exit the car park, turn right and cross the main road to a bridlepath signposted 'Ogden Clough' to pass the three-storey **Barley Green Farmhouse** with its interesting row of corbels. Proceed through circular gateposts, pass the **Nelson Water Works building** on the right and

rise up the grassy dam of the lower reservoir, where the metalled lane gives way to an unmade track. Continue straight ahead and join the Pendle Way as it leaves **Fell Wood** on the left; here you get your first tempting view of Pendle Hill up to the right. Keep straight ahead to the bottom of the upper reservoir, cross a stile and ascend the track beside the dam. Follow the

Pendle Way along the right-hand side of the reservoir and up **Ogden Clough**, passing through a kissing gate as you reach open country. The path is obvious to another kissing gate where you take the right of two options up a stony path that soon swings left and follows the contours.

② Cross the stream in **Boar Clough** and follow the waymarked path ahead as it detours slightly to avoid a badly eroded section. Its a steepish uphill climb for a while past a marker post to a more gentle climb on soft ground along a cairn marked route over **Barley Moor** to the trig pointed summit.

WHILE YOU'RE THERE ⓘ

Visit **Wycollar Country Park**, south east of Colne, where the centrepiece is ruined Wycollar Hall, believed to be Ferndean Manor in Charlotte Brontë's *Jane Eyre*. It's a beautiful, atmospheric location – a remote upland valley which survived industrialisation and depopulation. There are waymarked walks, a picnic site, tea room and craft shop.

WHAT TO LOOK FOR ⓘ

Pendle's thick blanket of peat supports significant types of **flora** including sedges, cranberry, crowberry, and if you're lucky, you might spot some cloudberry (sometimes known as mountain strawberry). Bearing fruit in June and July, look for the little orange clusters of berries.

---

③ Walk along the summit escarpment to a wall with a ladder stile. Stay on the right of the wall to a carved upright stone marking the **Pendle Way**, to strike sharp right and begin the quite steep descent down the stone stepped path.

④ Go right after the kissing gate at the bottom, signposted 'Barley', rounding the back of **Pendle House** to a yellow topped post and bear left through another gate. Drop down the meadow with a wall on the left and through a gate at the bottom leading into another meadow. Keep on down to a further gate leading to a farm building across a track. Turn right as signposted for a few paces then left through the grounds of **Brown House** to join a pretty tree-lined path between a stream and a wall.

⑤ Proceed through gates and over footbridges until you exit a narrow cobbled lane on to a metalled road and turn left through the lovely grounds of **Ing Ends**.

⑥ Soon cross a yellow waymarked footbridge on the right and bear left through a meadow and gates to pick up the stream on the left. On reaching the main road in Barley opposite the **Primitive Methodist church** turn right through the village to a Pendle Way marker leading you off the road, through the playground and park to the car park beyond.

WHERE TO EAT AND DRINK ⓘ

Barley has a selection of places for refreshments: the **Tea Rooms** offer home-made pies and broth with dumplings; the **Barley Mow** restaurant and the **Pendle Inn**, each offer appropriate facilities.

Laycock and Goose Eye

A varied walk, from intimate woodlands to the breezy moor-tops.

•DISTANCE•	8 miles (12.9km)
•MINIMUM TIME•	4hrs
•ASCENT / GRADIENT•	656ft (200m) ▲▲▲
•LEVEL OF DIFFICULTY•	🚶 🚶 🚶
•PATHS•	Good paths and tracks, take care with route finding, 8 stiles
•LANDSCAPE•	Wooded valley and heather moorland
•SUGGESTED MAP•	aqua3 OS Explorer OL21 South Pennines
•START / FINISH•	Grid reference: SE 035412
•DOG FRIENDLINESS•	Under control where sheep graze on sections of moorland
•PARKING•	In Laycock village, roadside parking at Keighley end of village, close to village hall
•PUBLIC TOILETS•	None on route
•CONTRIBUTOR•	John Morrison

BACKGROUND TO THE WALK

To the west of Keighley a tranche of moorland sits astride the border between Yorkshire and Lancashire. Here you can walk for miles without seeing another hiker – and perhaps with just curlew and grouse for company. When we think of textile mills, we tend to associate them with cramped towns full of smoking chimneys. But the earliest mills were sited in surprisingly rural locations, often in the little steep-sided valleys known as cloughs where fast-flowing becks and rivers could be dammed and diverted to turn the waterwheels. There are reminders, in wooded Newsholme Dean, that even a watercourse as small as Dean Beck could be harnessed to provide power to a cotton mill in Goose Eye. Weirs along the beck helped to maintain a good head of water, and one of the mill dams is now popular with anglers.

Laycock and Goose Eye

The village of Laycock contains a number of handsome old houses in the typical South Pennine style. While Laycock sits on the hillside, with good valley views, neighbouring Goose Eye nestles in a hollow. The village was originally called 'Goose Heights', which the local dialect contracted to 'Goose Ay', and thence to the name we know today. Lovers of real ale will already be familiar with the name, as this is the home of the Goose Eye Brewery.

Walk 40 Directions

① Walk through **Laycock**. Where the road narrows, go left down a track, **Roberts Street**. Pass terraced houses to join a walled path. You emerge on to a road, which you follow down into **Goose Eye**. Pass the **Turkey Inn**, the only pub on this walk. Just 50yds (46m) after you cross **Dean Beck**, take the steps on your right and re-cross the beck on a bridge. Follow the beck upstream and take a bridge on the right, across an empty channel.

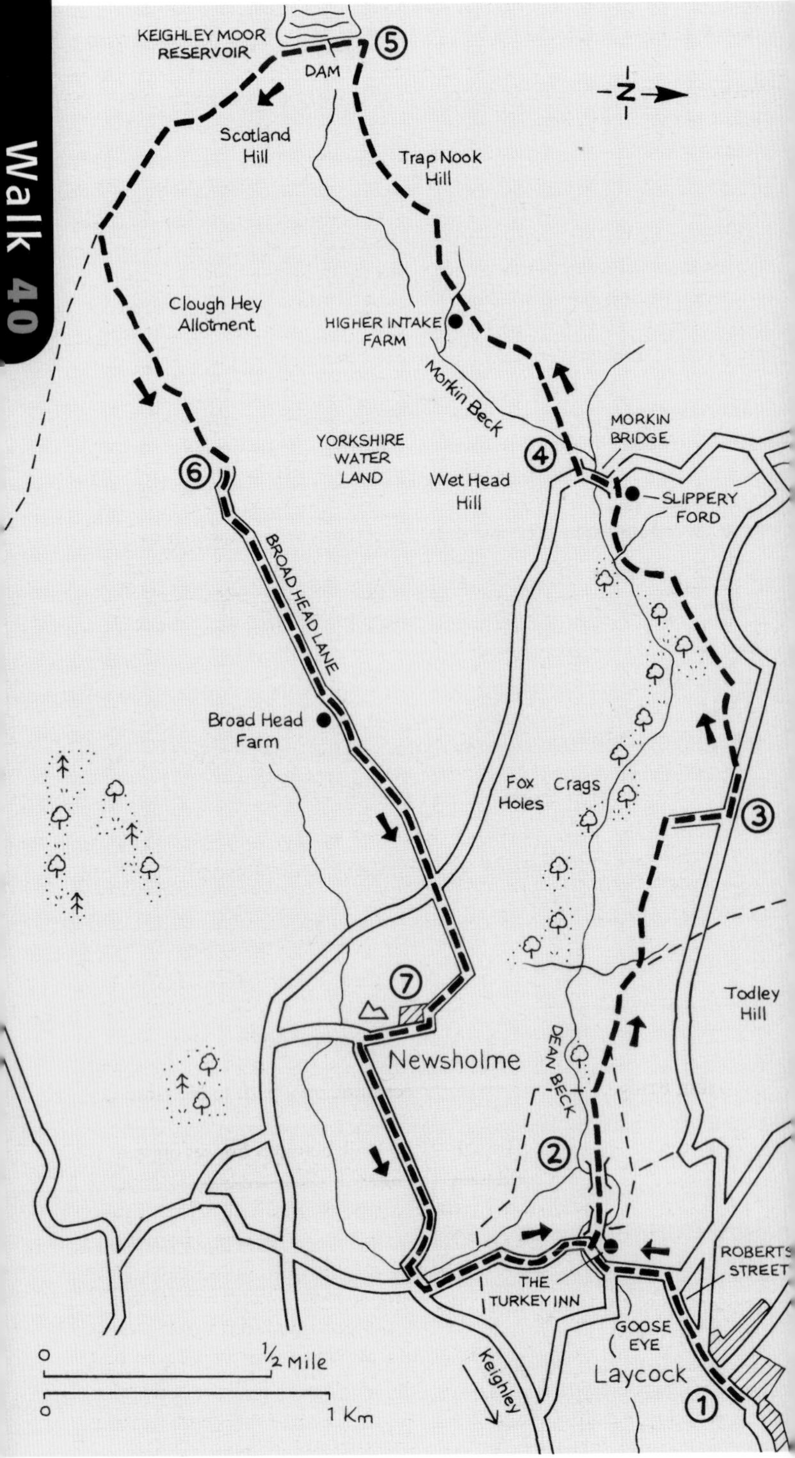

Walk 40

KEIGHLEY MOOR RESERVOIR

⑤

DAM

Scotland Hill

Trap Nook Hill

Clough Hey Allotment

HIGHER INTAKE FARM

Morkin Beck

MORKIN BRIDGE

④

SLIPPERY FORD

YORKSHIRE WATER LAND

Wet Head Hill

⑥

BROAD HEAD LANE

Broad Head Farm

Fox Holes

Crags

③

Todley Hill

⑦

Newsholme

DEAN BECK

②

THE TURKEY INN

ROBERTS STREET

Keighley

GOOSE EYE

Laycock

①

0   ½ Mile

0   1 Km

→ N →

② Pass a mill dam, soon enjoying easy walking, above the beck. Bear right up a paved path, levelling out between pasture and scrubland. Pass the rear of a farmhouse, and cross a stony track, to continue in the same direction, via a gate, along a track (signed to **Slippery Ford**). Continue uphill, through another gate and across a stream to a choice of tracks. Keep right, up a hollow way (or the adjacent path). Your path, soon paved, goes through a gate and up to meet a road.

③ Walk left, along the road, for 75yds (68m), before taking the access track on the left down to **Bottoms Farm**. Keep right of farm buildings to take a gate on the right. A path comes to a stile at the far end of a barn. Follow the path towards the head of the valley. Go through a gate to take a path, and stiles, across three fields in front of a farmhouse. At the bottom of the third field, you reach a point where two becks meet to form **Dean Beck**. Cross the beck in front of you, go through a gate and follow the other beck to a wall. Accompany the wall to the right, uphill, and take a gate on the left into the yard of **Slitheroford Farm**. Walk between some farm buildings and out to a road. Go left, down the road, and cross the beck once again at **Morkin Bridge**.

④ Bear immediately right through a gate on to Yorkshire Water land and follow a good metalled track uphill. You can lengthen your stride

WHERE TO EAT AND DRINK ⓘ
The **Turkey Inn**, towards the beginning of the walk in Goose Eye, is a splendid village pub, with a reputation for good food that extents much further afield.

as the track traverses heather moorland, and passes a lonely farm, **Higher Intake**. The highest point of your walk is soon reached: **Keighley Moor Reservoir**.

⑤ Walk left, across the top of the dam. At the far end of the reservoir ignore the more obvious track to the right. Keep left of a concrete post to join a grassy moorland track, slightly downhill. The path becomes indistinct at a boggy section. Just keep straight ahead to meet a wall. Follow the wall for 150yds (138m) before going through a gateway in the wall. Bear half right to cross a line of grouse butts and locate a distinct but narrow path through the heather. Follow this path to a wall stile where you join a walled track heading right.

WHILE YOU'RE THERE ⓘ
Visit **Cliffe Castle Museum**, set in an attractive hillside park on Spring Gardens Lane. It was built in the 1880s as a mansion for a mill owner, and is now Keighley's museum, specialising in natural history and geology.

⑥ Follow this track, **Broad Head Lane**, soon leaving the moorland behind. The track is metalled once you reach an isolated group of houses. Cross a road by a farm and continue on a path to **Newsholme**.

⑦ Walk between houses on to a metalled lane, following it down to the next group of houses. Take a lane on your left, which soon becomes a track. Cross a beck and meet a road. Walk left down into **Goose Eye**. Walk through the village and steeply up the road. The road bends sharp right, then sharp left. Take a path to the right here, which delivers you back into **Laycock**.

Haworth's Brontë Moors

Across the wild Pennine moors to the romantic ruin of Top Withins.

•DISTANCE•	7½ miles (12.1km)
•MINIMUM TIME•	3hrs 30min
•ASCENT / GRADIENT•	650ft (200m) ▲▲▲
•LEVEL OF DIFFICULTY•	🚶🚶 🚶🚶
•PATHS•	Well-signed and easy to follow, 2 stiles
•LANDSCAPE•	Open moorland
•SUGGESTED MAP•	aqua3 OS Explorer OL21 South Pennines
•START / FINISH•	Grid reference: SE 029373
•DOG FRIENDLINESS•	Under control near sheep on open moorland
•PARKING•	Pay-and-display car park, near Brontë Parsonage
•PUBLIC TOILETS•	Central Park, Haworth
•CONTRIBUTOR•	John Morrison

BACKGROUND TO THE WALK

Who could have imagined, when the Revd Patrick Brontë became curate of the Church of St Michael and All Angels in 1820, that the little gritstone town of Haworth would become a literary Mecca to rival Grasmere and Stratford-upon-Avon? But it has, and visitors flock here in great numbers: some to gain some insights into the works of Charlotte, Emily and Anne, others just to enjoy a day out.

If the shy sisters could see the Haworth of today, they would recognise the steep, cobbled main street. But they would no doubt be amazed to see the tourist industry that's built up to exploit their names and literary reputations. They would recognise the Georgian parsonage too. Now a museum, it has been painstakingly restored to reflect the lives of the Brontës and the rooms are filled with their personal treasures.

That three such prodigious talents should be found within a single family is remarkable enough. To have created such towering works as *Jane Eyre* and *Wuthering Heights* while living in what was a bleakly inhospitable place is almost beyond belief. The public were unprepared for this trio of lady novelists, which is why all the books published during their lifetimes bore the androgynous pen-names of Currer, Ellis and Acton Bell.

From the day that Patrick Brontë came to Haworth with his wife and six children, tragedy was never far away. His wife died the following year and two daughters did not live to adulthood. His only son Branwell succumbed to drink and drugs; Anne and Emily died aged 29 and 30 respectively. Charlotte, alone, lived long enough to marry. But after just one year of marriage – to her father's curate – she too fell ill and died in 1855, at the age of 38. Revd Brontë survived them all, living to the ripe old age of 84.

Tourism is no recent development; by the middle of the 19th century the first literary pilgrims were finding their way to Haworth. No matter how crowded this little town becomes (and those who value their solitude should avoid visiting on a sunny summer weekend) it is always possible to escape to the moors that surround the town. You can follow, literally, in the footsteps of the three sisters as they sought freedom and inspiration, away from the stifling confines of the parsonage and the adjacent graveyard. As you explore these inhospitable moors, you'll get a greater insight into the literary world of the Brontës than those who stray no further than the souvenir shops and tea rooms of Haworth.

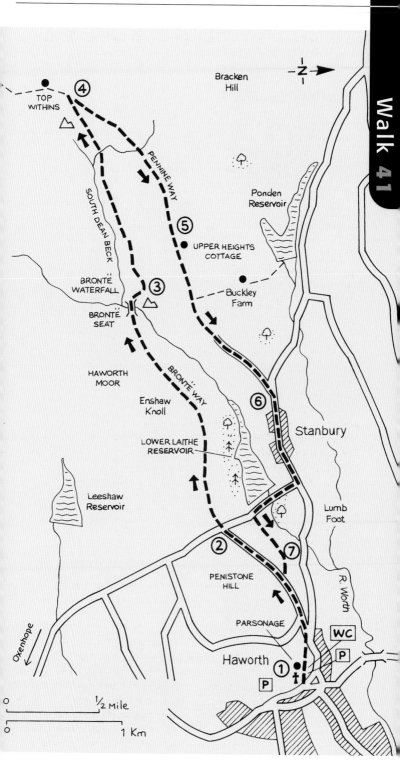

Bracken
Hill

TOP
WITHINS ④

PENNINE WAY

Ponden
Reservoir

⑤

UPPER HEIGHTS
COTTAGE

SOUTH DEAN BECK

Buckley
Farm

BRONTË
WATERFALL ③

BRONTË
SEAT

HAWORTH
MOOR

BRONTË WAY

Enshaw
Knoll

⑥

Stanbury

LOWER LAITHE
RESERVOIR

Leeshaw
Reservoir

Lumb
Foot

②

⑦

R. Worth

PENISTONE
HILL

Oxenhope

PARSONAGE

WC

P

Haworth ①

P

0 ½ Mile

0 1 Km

Walk 41

Walk 41 Directions

① Take the cobbled lane up past the parsonage, signed to **Haworth Moor**. The lane soon becomes a paved field path that leads to the **Haworth–Stanbury** road. Walk left along the road and, after just 75yds (68m), take a left fork, signed to **Penistone Hill**. Continue along this quiet road to a T-junction.

② Take the track straight ahead, soon signed '**Brontë Way** and **Top Withins**', gradually descending to **South Dean Beck** where, within a few paces of the stone bridge, you'll find the **Brontë Waterfall** and **Brontë Seat** (a stone that resembles a chair). Cross the bridge and climb steeply uphill to a three-way sign.

WHILE YOU'RE THERE ⓘ
At the bottom of that famous cobbled street is Haworth Station, on the restored **Keighley and Worth Valley Railway**. Take a steam train journey on Britain's last remaining complete branch line railway. Or browse through the books and railway souvenirs at the station shop.

③ Keep left, uphill, on a paved path signed '**Top Withins**'. The path levels out to accompany a wall. Cross a beck on stepping stones; a steep uphill climb brings you to a waymarker by a ruined building. Take a short detour of 200yds (183m), left, uphill, to visit the ruin of **Top Withins**, possibly the inspiration for Wuthering Heights.

④ Turn right at the waymarker, on a paved path, downhill, signed to **Stanbury** and **Haworth**; you are now joining the **Pennine Way**. You have a broad, easily-followed track across the wide expanse of wild Pennine moorland.

⑤ Pass a white farmhouse – **Upper Heights Cottage** – then bear immediately left at a fork of tracks (still signed here as the **Pennine Way**). Walk past another building, **Lower Heights Farm**. After 500yds (456m) you come to another fork: where the **Pennine Way** veers off to the left, you should continue on the track straight ahead, signed to **Stanbury** and **Haworth**. Follow the track to meet a road near the village of **Stanbury**.

WHERE TO EAT AND DRINK ⓘ
The **Black Bull** is Haworth's most famous public house, standing in the little cobbled square at the top of the steep main street. This is where Branwell Brontë came to drown his sorrows, and tried to forget the trauma of having such clever sisters. These days you can also have a sandwich, or a snack... or go for the Full Brontë.

⑥ Bear right along the road through **Stanbury**, then take the first road on the right, signed to **Oxenhope**, and cross the dam of **Lower Laithe Reservoir**. Immediately beyond the dam, bear left on a road that is soon reduced to a track uphill, to meet a road by **Haworth Cemetery**.

⑦ From here you retrace your outward route: walk left along the road, soon taking a gap stile on the right, to follow the paved field path back into **Haworth**.

WHAT TO LOOK FOR ⓘ
The Brontës are 'big in Japan'. It seems that the Japanese have an almost insatiable appetite to learn about the sisters' lives and books. So don't be surprised to find that a lot of signs in the town – and on the walk to Top Withins too – are written in English and Japanese. Strange but true.

Walk 42

Bingley and the St Ives Estate

Great views of Airedale from a viewpoint known as the Druid's Altar.

•DISTANCE•	5½ miles (8.8km)
•MINIMUM TIME•	3hrs
•ASCENT / GRADIENT•	525ft (160m) ▲▲▲
•LEVEL OF DIFFICULTY•	🚶🚶 🚶🚶 🚶
•PATHS•	Good paths and tracks throughout, 2 stiles
•LANDSCAPE•	Woodland, park and river
•SUGGESTED MAP•	aqua3 OS Explorer 288 Bradford & Huddersfield
•START / FINISH•	Grid reference: SE 107393
•DOG FRIENDLINESS•	Can be off lead on St Ives Estate
•PARKING•	Car parks in Bingley
•PUBLIC TOILETS•	In Myrtle Park, Bingley
•CONTRIBUTOR•	John Morrison

BACKGROUND TO THE WALK

Sitting astride both the River Aire and the Leeds and Liverpool Canal, in a steep-sided valley, Bingley is a typical West Yorkshire town. With its locks, wharfs and plethora of mills, the town grew in size and importance during the 19th century as the textile trades expanded. But Bingley's pre-eminence did not begin with the Industrial Revolution; it is, in fact, one of the county's oldest settlements, with its market charter being granted by King John as far back as 1212.

In keeping with its age, Bingley has a number of splendid old buildings, such as the town hall, parish church, butter cross, the old market hall and the Old White Horse, a venerable coaching inn. Ancient and modern sit side-by-side in Bingley, which has more than its fair share of architectural monstrosities, dating from more recent times. The headquarters of the Bradford & Bingley Building Society is perhaps a case in point.

Halliwell Sutcliffe, author of such books as *The Striding Dales* and *By Moor and Fell*, lived in Bingley while his father was headmaster of the town's Grammar School.

River Aire

The River Aire rises close to the village of Malham, in the limestone dales of North Yorkshire, and flows past Bingley. By the time it joins the Ouse and decants into the Humber Estuary it has been one of the hardest worked watercourses in Yorkshire. When the textile trades were at their height, the Aire was both a source of power for the woollen mills and a convenient dumping ground for industrial waste. But, like so many other West Yorkshire rivers, the water quality is now greatly improved.

For part of this walk, you will be exploring the St Ives Estate which, from 1636, was owned by one of Bingley's most prominent families, the Ferrands. It was William Ferrand who, during the 1850s, landscaped the estate and created many of the footpaths and tracks that climb steeply up through the woods. The view from the top of the hill is ample reward for your efforts. From the gritstone outcrop known – somewhat fancifully – as the

Druid's Altar, you have a splendid panorama across Bingley and the valley of the River Aire. There is an inscription on Lady Blantyre's Rock, which you will pass on the later stages of this walk. It commemorates William Ferrand's mother-in-law. Lady Blantyre often used to sit in the shade of this rock and read a book. It's a splendid notion: a monument to idleness. Near by is an obelisk with a dedication to William Ferrand himself. St Ives, a little wooded oasis on urban Bingley's doorstep, is now looked after by Bradford city council on behalf of local people.

Walk 42 Directions

① Walk downhill from the centre of **Bingley**, towards the church. Go left at the traffic lights, passing the **Old White Horse** pub, on to **Millgate**. Cross the River Aire and take the first right, **Ireland Street**, veering right past industrial buildings to join a riverside track.

Very soon you seem to have swapped town for country. Bear right in front of **Ravenroyd Farm**, to pass between other farm buildings and continue on a walled track. Pass another house, **Cophurst**, and through pasture, with thick woodland on your left.

② The track skirts a hillock and approaches **Marley Farm**.

Go through a metal gate on the left, to continue on a field path that soon emerges on to a more substantial track. Bear left, immediately, by **Blakey Cottage**, on a setted (paved) track uphill. You soon gain height, passing two more farms, with views of **Airedale** opening up on the right. The track bears left and, after 100yds (91m), left again. At this point look for a stile ahead of you and take a narrow path that climbs steeply up through bracken. Keep left at a fork of tracks to the top of the hill to enjoy level walking with a wall on your right. Cross a track to arrive, just 100yds (91m) further on, at a rocky outcrop, known as the **Druid's Altar**, which offers splendid views.

③ Bear right, after the rocks, to come to a meeting of tracks. Go through a gap in the wall ahead, on to a walled track that leads into the **St Ives Estate**. Bear immediately to the right, through a gap stile in a wall, to take a path with woodland to your right and open fields to your left. After ½ mile (800m) you come to a kissing gate in the wall on your right, but your route is left here, into the woods and between golf fairways. At a choice of paths ahead, take the right-hand option, soon having a wall on your left and heather heathland on your right. Follow the path downhill, passing **Lady Blantyre's Rock**.

④ Ignoring side-tracks, follow the path downhill, past rhododendrons, to **Coppice Pond**. Join a metalled road to bear left, soon passing a stable block, golf clubhouse and the house itself, **St Ives**.

⑤ Bear right past the house, to follow the house's drive downhill. Just 100yds (91m) before the road,

> **WHILE YOU'RE THERE** ⓘ
> Next to Bingley is the little town of **Cottingley** where, in 1917, two young girls took photographs of fairies by Cottingley Beck. Despite the fairies looking like paper cut-outs, the pictures were 'authenticated' by Arthur Conan Doyle, creator of the fiercely logical Sherlock Holmes. Pay a visit to Cottingley Beck, and listen out for the beating of tiny wings...

take a path, left, through woodland. Keep right where the track forks, to reach the B6429, the Bingley to Cullingworth road. Cross it and continue downhill on narrow **Beckfoot Lane**. After houses the lane becomes an unmade track leading down to a delectable spot: here you will find **Beckfoot Farm**, in a wooded setting by **Harden Beck**, with a ford and an old packhorse bridge that dates back to 1723.

⑥ Cross the bridge and bear left at **Beckfoot Farm**, to find allotments on your left. Where the allotments end, take a path to the left which leads to a metal footbridge over the **River Aire** and into **Myrtle Park**. Cross the park to arrive once again in the centre of **Bingley**.

Extending the Walk
While you're in **Bingley** you can extend the walk by dropping down to the canal and walking up to the **Five Rise Locks**. On your way back, **Treacle Cock Alley** will bring you out by the parish church.

> **WHERE TO EAT AND DRINK** ⓘ
> The oldest pub in Bingley is the 16th-century **Old White Horse Inn**, which you pass early on in this walk. It has oodles of character: that patina of age just can't be faked (no matter how hard the big pub chains try).

Shipley Glen's Tramway and Baildon Moor

A glimpse of moorland and a traditional rural playground for the mill workers of Shipley and Saltaire.

•DISTANCE•	4 miles (6.4km)
•MINIMUM TIME•	2hrs
•ASCENT / GRADIENT•	492ft (150m) ▲▲▲
•LEVEL OF DIFFICULTY•	🚶 🚶🚶 🚶🚶🚶
•PATHS•	Moor and field paths, 1 stile
•LANDSCAPE•	Moorland, fields and gritstone rocks
•SUGGESTED MAP•	aqua3 OS Explorer 288 Bradford & Huddersfield
•START / FINISH•	Grid reference: SE 132389
•DOG FRIENDLINESS•	Can be off leads except in Saltaire
•PARKING•	On Glen Road, between Bracken Hall Countryside Centre and Old Glen House pub
•PUBLIC TOILETS•	At Bracken Hall Countryside Centre
•CONTRIBUTOR•	John Morrison

BACKGROUND TO THE WALK

For the people of Shipley and Saltaire, Baildon Moor has traditionally represented a taste of the countryside on their doorsteps. Millhands could leave the mills and cramped terraced streets behind, and breathe clean Pennine air. They could listen to the song of the skylark and the bubbling cry of the curlew. There were heather moors to tramp across, gritstone rocks to scramble up and, at Shipley Glen, springy sheep-grazed turf on which to spread out a picnic blanket. There was also a funfair to visit – not a little funfair, like there still is today – but a veritable theme park.

Towards the end of the 19th century Shipley Glen was owned by a Colonel Maude, who created a number of attractions. Visitors could enjoy the sundry delights of the Switchback Railway, Marsden's Menagerie, the Horse Tramway and the Aerial Runway. More sedate pleasures could be found at the Camera Obscura, the boating lake in the Japanese garden, and the Temperance Tea Room and Coffee House.

Sam Wilson, a local entrepreneur, played his own part in developing Shipley Glen. In 1895 he created the Shipley Glen Tramway. Saltaire people could now stroll through Roberts Park, past the steely-gazed statue of Sir Titus Salt, and enjoy the tram-ride to the top of the glen. Thousands of people would clamber, each weekend, on to the little cable-hauled 'toast-rack' cars. As one car went up the hill, another car would descend on an adjacent track.

In commercial terms, the heyday of Shipley Glen was during the Edwardian era. On busy days as many as 17,000 people would take the tramway up to the pleasure gardens. Losing out to more sophisticated entertainments, however, Shipley Glen went into a slow decline. Most of the attractions are now gone, but not all. You can still ride the Aerial Runway (though it's not exactly a white-knuckle ride) and spend some money at the little funfair. Best of all, you can still take the tramway – which runs every day from May to September, with more restrictive operation during the winter.

The Old Glen House is still a popular pub, though the Temperance Tea Room and Coffee House have been transformed into the Bracken Hall Countryside Centre. Local people still enjoy the freedom of the heather moorland. Despite all the changes, Shipley Glen retains a stubbornly old-fashioned air, and is all the better for it.

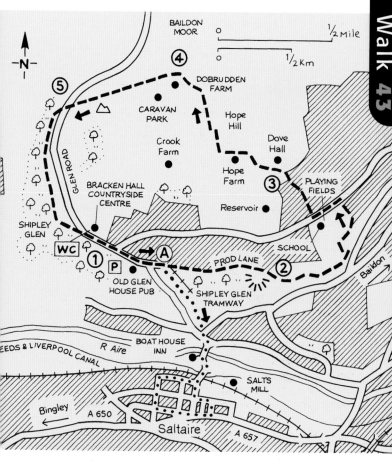

Walk 43 Directions

① Walk down **Glen Road**, passing the **Old Glen House** pub. Continue as the road becomes **Prod Lane**, signed as a cul-de-sac. Pass the tiny funfair and the entrance to the **Shipley Glen Tramway**. Where the road ends, keep straight ahead to locate an enclosed path to the right of a house. Follow this path, with houses on your left, and woodland to your right. As you come to a metal barrier, ignore a path to the left. Keep straight on downhill. 100yds (91m) beyond the barrier, you have a choice of paths; bear left here, uphill, soon getting good views over **Saltaire**, **Shipley** and the **Aire Valley**.

② Beyond the woodland, you walk beneath a quarried sandstone cliff. When you come to an open area, with panoramic views, take a set of stone steps, with metal handrails, up to the top of the cliff. Bear right on a path between chain-link fences, which takes you around school playing fields, to meet a road. Walk left along the road for 150yds (138m). When you are level with the school on your left, cross the road and take a narrow, enclosed path on the right, between houses. Walk gradually uphill, crossing a road in a housing estate and picking up the enclosed path again. Soon, at a stile, you emerge into pasture.

> **WHAT TO LOOK FOR** ⓘ
> Call in at the **Bracken Hall Countryside Centre** on Glen Road, which has a number of interesting displays about the history of Shipley Glen, its flora and its fauna. There are also temporary exhibitions on particular themes, interactive features and a programme of children's activities throughout the year. The gift shop sells maps, guides, natural history books and ice creams.

③ Go half left, uphill, to a kissing gate at the top-left corner of the field. Before you reach the farm you see ahead, join the access track, walking past the buildings on a cinder track until a metal gate bars your way. Go right here, through a wooden gate, on a path between walls. Beyond the next gate you come out on to **Baildon Moor**. Your path is clear, following a wall to your left. Keep straight on, as the wall curves to the left, towards the

> **WHERE TO EAT AND DRINK** ⓘ
> The **Boat House Inn**, next to the River Aire, was Sir Titus Salt's private boathouse – built in 1871. Since he wouldn't allow any public houses in Saltaire, he may be turning in his grave to see his boathouse transformed into a rather handsome pub today. You can enjoy your meal or drink on a little terrace overlooking the river.

> **WHILE YOU'RE THERE** ⓘ
> Make sure to visit **Salts Mill**, a giant of a building on a truly epic scale. At the height of production 3,000 people worked here. There were 1,200 looms clattering away, weaving as much as 30,000 yards of cloth every working day. The mill is a little quieter these days – with a permanent exhibition of artworks by David Hockney, another of Bradford's most famous sons.

next farm (and caravan park). Cross a metalled farm track and curve left to follow the boundary wall of **Dobrudden Farm**.

④ Walk gradually downhill towards **Bingley** in the valley. When the wall bears left, keep straight ahead, through bracken, more steeply downhill. Cross a metalled track and carry on down to meet **Glen Road** again.

⑤ Follow the path along the rocky edge of wooded **Shipley Glen** leading you back to the **Bracken Hall Countryside Centre** and your car.

Extending the Walk
It's worth the detour from Point Ⓐ, down the **Shipley Glen Tramway**, across the river and canal to the model industrial village of **Saltaire**.

Walk 44

Oxenhope and the Worth Valley Railway

A moorland round and a return to the age of steam.

•DISTANCE•	6 miles (9.7km)
•MINIMUM TIME•	3hrs
•ASCENT / GRADIENT•	492ft (150m) ▲▲▲
•LEVEL OF DIFFICULTY•	ẋẋ ẋẋ ẋẋ
•PATHS•	Good paths and tracks, 6 stiles
•LANDSCAPE•	Upland scenery, moor and pasture
•SUGGESTED MAP•	aqua3 OS Explorer OL21 South Pennines
•START / FINISH•	Grid reference: SE 033354
•DOG FRIENDLINESS•	Keep on lead along country lanes
•PARKING•	Street parking in Oxenhope, near Keighley and Worth Valley Railway station
•PUBLIC TOILETS•	None on route
•CONTRIBUTOR•	John Morrison

BACKGROUND TO THE WALK

Oxenhope is at the end of the line in more ways than one. As well as being the terminus of the Keighley and Worth Valley Railway, Oxenhope is the last village in the Worth Valley. To the north are Haworth and Keighley; going south, into Calderdale and Hebden Bridge, requires you to gear down for a scenic drive over the lonely heights of Cock Hill.

Oxenhope was a farming community that expanded, like many other villages in West Yorkshire, with the textile industry. The mills, however, have mostly disappeared, leaving the village to commuters who work in nearby towns. Apart from the railway, the village is best known for the Oxenhope Straw Race, held each year on the first Sunday in July. Competitors have to carry a bale of straw around the village, while drinking as much beer as possible. Whoever finishes this assault course first, it is the local charities that benefit most.

Keighley and Worth Valley Railway

The Keighley and Worth Valley line, running for 5 miles (8km) from Keighley to Oxenhope, is one of the longest established private railways in the country, and the last remaining complete branch line. It was built in 1867, funded by local mill owners, but the trains were run by the Midland Railway to link to the main Leeds–Skipton line at Keighley.

When the line fell victim to Dr Beeching's axe in 1962, local rail enthusiasts banded together in opposition to the closure. The preservation society bought the line: a pioneering example of rail privatisation. Thus began a major restoration of the line and its stations. Ingrow Station, for example, had been so badly vandalised that a complete station was 'transported' to the site stone by stone from Foulridge in Lancashire. Built to the typical Midland style, it now blends in well with the other stations on the line. By 1968 the society began running regular trains. Steam trains run every weekend throughout the year, and daily in summer. But the line doesn't just cater for tourists; locals in the Worth Valley appreciate the diesel services into Keighley which operate on almost 200 days per year.

Walk 44

The line runs through the heart of Brontë country, with stations at Oxenhope, Haworth, Oakworth, Danems, Ingrow and Keighley. The stations are a particular delight: fully restored, gas-lit and redolent of the age of steam. So when Edith Nesbitt's classic children's novel, *The Railway Children*, was being filmed in 1970, the Keighley and Worth Valley Railway was a natural choice of setting. And Oakworth Station – a splendid example of an Edwardian station, complete with enamel advertising signs – is the one used in the film. Everyone who has seen the film (it's the one with Jenny Agutter in and it seems to be etched deeply into the national psyche) will enjoy revisiting the much-loved locations.

Walk 44 Directions

① From the entrance of **Oxenhope Station** take the minor road to the left, up to the A6033. Cross the road and take **Dark Lane** ahead, a sunken lane that goes steeply uphill. Follow this track to a road. Go right here, downhill, to join the **Denholme road** (B6141). Walk left along the road, up to the **Dog and Gun** pub, where you turn right on to **Sawood Lane**.

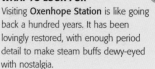

> ### WHERE TO EAT AND DRINK
> At about the half-way point, this walk passes the **Waggon & Horses**, an isolated pub on the Hebden Bridge Road out of Oxenhope. The pub enjoys great views over the valley towards Haworth and the moors, and has a good reputation for its food. If you decide to take the train there's an excellent café at **Oxenhope Station**, appropriately enough in a stationary British Rail buffet car.

② At **Coblin Farm**, your route becomes a rough track. Go through a gate to join a metalled road to the right, uphill, signed **Brontë Way**. After 100yds (91m), when the road accesses **Thornton Moor Reservoir**, walk straight ahead on an unmade track. Go through a gate into rough pasture, ignoring the **Brontë Way** sign to the right.

③ At a fork, just 50yds (46m) further on, keep right as the track goes downhill towards a transmission mast on the mid-horizon. Pass a clump of trees, and cross a watercourse before descending to a minor road.

④ Go right here to pass a cattle grid and the mast. 150yds (138m) beyond the mast, as the road begins a steep descent, take a wall stile on

the left. Go through another wall stile, to walk left, uphill, on a broad, walled track that deposits you at the **Waggon and Horses** pub.

⑤ Cross the road and take a track between gateposts, which bears right, steeply downhill. Where it bears sharp right again, after 300yds (274m), take a stile to the left, by a gate. Follow a wall downhill to take three stiles in succession; at the bottom you meet a walled path. Go left here, cross a stream, and continue uphill to arrive at the entrance to **Lower Fold Farm**.

⑥ Follow the farm track to the right; turn right again, 20yds (18m) further on, at the end of a cottage, to join a metalled track. The track soon bears right above **Leeshaw Reservoir** and makes a gradual descent. Pass a mill to meet a road.

> ### WHAT TO LOOK FOR
> Visiting **Oxenhope Station** is like going back a hundred years. It has been lovingly restored, with enough period detail to make steam buffs dewy-eyed with nostalgia.

⑦ Cross the road and take the track ahead (signed to **Marsh**). Keep right of the first house, on a narrow walled path, then a paved path. Pass through the courtyard of a house as the path goes left, then right, and through a kissing gate. Follow a path between a wall and a fence to meet a walled lane. Go right here, passing houses, then on a field path to meet a road. Go right here and back down into **Oxenhope**.

> ### WHILE YOU'RE THERE
> Take a trip to Haworth and back on the **Keighley and Worth Valley Railway**, and relive the great days of steam. You can return on foot along the Worth Way.

Walk 45

Discovering the Rural Side of Leeds

From the bustle of the city to the heart of the country.

•DISTANCE•	5 miles (8km)
•MINIMUM TIME•	2hrs 30min
•ASCENT / GRADIENT•	98ft (30m) ▲▲ ▲ ▲
•LEVEL OF DIFFICULTY•	👫 👫👫 👫👫
•PATHS•	Urban ginnels, parkland and woodland paths, 2 stiles
•LANDSCAPE•	Mostly woodland
•SUGGESTED MAP•	aqua3 OS Explorers 289 Leeds; 297 Lower Wharfedale
•START•	Grid reference: SE 294352 (on Explorer 289)
•FINISH•	Grid reference: SE 270402 (on Explorer 297)
•DOG FRIENDLINESS•	Good, but watch for traffic early on
•PARKING•	Free parking on Raglan Road, just off the A660, at eastern end of Woodhouse Moor
•PUBLIC TOILETS•	Meanwood Park
•CONTRIBUTOR•	John Morrison

BACKGROUND TO THE WALK

This, the only linear walk in the book, is a splendid ramble, surprisingly rural in aspect throughout, even though it begins just a stone's throw from the bustling heart of Leeds. You start among the terraces of red-brick houses that are so typical of the city, and five minutes later you are in delightful woodland.

Linking with the Dales Way

The walk follows the first 5 miles (8km) of the Dales Way link path from Leeds to Ilkley (the long distance walk's official starting point). This link path begins at Woodhouse Moor – where fairs and circuses have long pitched their tents – so we shall do the same. The path follows first Woodhouse Ridge, then the Hollies and the Meanwood Valley, the path cocooned against creeping suburbia by a slim sliver of woodland. The route is also being promoted as the Meanwood Valley Trail, so there are waymarkers to guide you at every point of indecision.

Leeds is fortunate to have so many parks within the city limits: long-established green spaces such as Roundhay Park, and newer parks created from 'brownfield' sites. The first few miles of this walk are through some of this pleasant parkland. Then, having crossed beneath the Leeds Ring Road, you have the more natural surroundings of Adel Woods to enjoy.

The walk finishes near Adel church, dedicated to St John the Baptist. Though small, it is one of the most perfectly proportioned Norman churches in the country, having been built about 1170. The ornamental stone carving is noteworthy – especially the four arches framing the doorway. From here there's a reliable bus service back to Woodhouse Moor. To lengthen the walk by 1½ miles (2.4km), don't turn left down Stairfoot Lane, but take the track ahead, and turn left when you come to King Lane. This brings you out at Golden Acre Park (➤ Walk 36), near Bramhope (on the same bus route for getting back to Leeds).

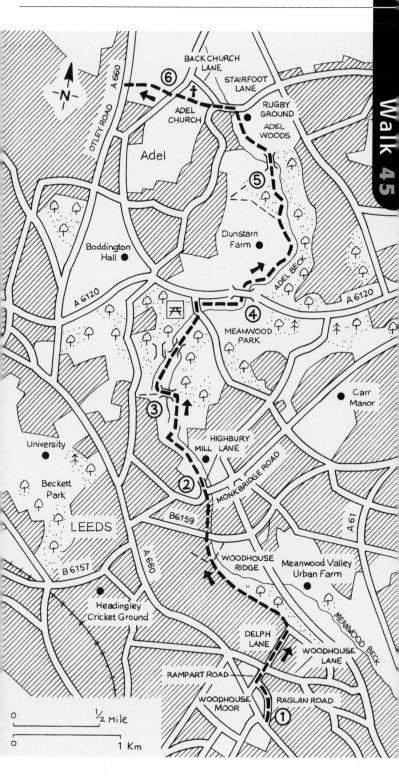

Walk 45 **Directions**

① Walk down **Raglan Road** and turn right on to **Rampart Road**. Cross **Woodhouse Lane**, and walk ahead up **Delph Lane**. When the road ends at a wall, take a gate and walk left along **Woodhouse Ridge**. Don't be side-tracked; keep to the obvious path, with woodland to your right and a high wall to your left. At a barrier take the middle option, then up and down some steps, and across a road, continuing in the same direction. This ginnel emerges at **Monkbridge Road**.

② Cross the road, and take **Highbury Lane** ahead – soon recovering the path, which now accompanies **Meanwood Beck**. As you pass a mill follow a path first left, then right, beyond the mill dam. Walk between allotments and past a cricket ground, to join a road for just 100yds (91m). Bear right, in front of a post-box, through stone gateposts, to enter **Meanwood Park**. Bear left, beyond a small car park, on a metalled lane through the park, to a short row of terraced houses known as **Hustlers Row**.

③ Keep left of the houses as the lane becomes a stony track. Cross **Meanwood Beck** on a footbridge, bearing right at a fork of tracks to follow the beck into woodland. Cross a side-beck, to have this watercourse on your left and the beck on your right. Ignore side-tracks and a footbridge on the left to arrive at a double bridge. Cross the beck to your right, and continue to follow its course. Go right at a stile 50yds (46m) beyond the bridge, and immediately left to follow a field-edge path. Meet a road by a picnic site and

information panel. Go left along the road. Just 20yds (18m) from the ring road, go right on a metalled track which soon continues as a path. Beyond a paddock go left through a tunnel beneath the road.

④ Take steps, at the far end, on to a path that follows **Adel Beck**. Keep left of the next pile of boulders, on a path through woodland. After a small pond go right, downhill, alongside an aqueduct into **Adel Woods**. Keep right at the next fork and cross a stony track to another meeting of tracks.

⑤ Walk straight ahead, cross the beck on a stone bridge, and take steps uphill to a pond. Keep to the right-hand path, past a rugby ground – soon reaching a car park and a minor road, **Stairfoot Lane**. Go left down the road; this sunken lane soon rises to a junction. Go right on to **Back Church Lane**. When the road bears right, keep straight on to follow the wall on your left and access a track that takes you straight to **Adel church**.

⑥ Walk past the church and leave the churchyard by a collection of coffins and millstones. Cross the road and take a field path opposite. Bear half left across the next field to the **Otley Road** (A660). Turn left to find a bus stop, opposite a petrol station, for the bus back to **Woodhouse Moor**, in Leeds.

WHERE TO EAT AND DRINK   ⓘ
There are several pubs just off-route during this walk. But the simplest option is to wait until the finishing point, where you will find the **Lawnswood Arms**. Your car is parked close to the university, so you will find cheap and cheerful curry houses nearby, and some characterful city pubs.

Jumble Hole and Colden Clough

Textile history from cottage industry to the mills of bustling Hebden Bridge.

•DISTANCE•	5½ miles (8.8km)
•MINIMUM TIME•	3hrs
•ASCENT / GRADIENT•	722ft (220m) ▲▲▲
•LEVEL OF DIFFICULTY•	👫 👫 👫
•PATHS•	Good paths, 13 stiles
•LANDSCAPE•	Steep-sided valleys, fields and woodland
•SUGGESTED MAP•	aqua3 OS Explorer OL21 South Pennines
•START / FINISH•	Grid reference: SD 992272
•DOG FRIENDLINESS•	Good most of the way, but livestock in upland fields
•PARKING•	Pay-and-display car parks in Hebden Bridge
•PUBLIC TOILETS•	Hebden Bridge and Heptonstall
•CONTRIBUTOR•	John Morrison

BACKGROUND TO THE WALK

This walk links the little town of Hebden Bridge with the old hand-weaving village of Heptonstall, using sections of a waymarked walk, the Calderdale Way. The hill village of Heptonstall is by far the older settlement and was, in its time, an important centre of the textile trade. A cursory look at a map shows Heptonstall to be at the hub of a complex network of old trackways, mostly used by packhorse trains carrying wool and cotton. And Heptonstall's Cloth Hall, where cloth was bought and sold, dates back to the 16th century. At this time Hebden Bridge was little more than a river crossing on an old packhorse causey.

Wheels of Industry

Heptonstall's importance came at the time when textiles were, literally, a cottage industry, with spinning and weaving being undertaken in isolated farmhouses. When the processes began to be mechanised, during the Industrial Revolution, Heptonstall, with no running water to power the waterwheels, was left high and dry. As soon as spinning and weaving developed on a truly industrial scale, communities sprang up wherever there was a ready supply of running water. So the town of Hebden Bridge was established in the valley, at the meeting of two rivers: the Calder and Hebden Water. The handsome 16th-century packhorse bridge that gives the town its name still spans Hebden Water.

At one time there were more than 30 mills in Hebden Bridge, their tall chimneys belching thick smoke into the Calder Valley. It used to be said that the only time you could see the town from the surrounding hills was during Wakes Week, the millhands' traditional holiday. The town's speciality was cotton: mostly hard-wearing fustian and corduroy. With Hebden Bridge being hemmed in by hills, and the mills occupying much of the available land on the valley bottom, the workers' houses had to be built up the steep slopes. An ingenious solution to the problem was to build 'top and bottom' houses, one dwelling on top of another. They can be viewed to best effect on the last leg of the walk, which offers a birds-eye view over the town. Few looms clatter today and Hebden Bridge has reinvented itself as the 'capital' of Upper Calderdale, as a place to enjoy a day out. The town is known for its excellent walking country, bohemian population, trips along the Rochdale Canal by horse-drawn narrowboats and its summer arts festival. Jumble Hole Clough is a typical South Pennine steep-sided, wooded valley. Though a tranquil scene today, this little valley was once a centre of industry, with four mills exploiting the fast-flowing beck. You can see remains of all these mills, and some of their mill ponds, on this walk; but the most intriguing relic is Staups Mill, now an evocative ruin, near the top of Jumble Hole Clough.

APPLE TREE FARM
HIPPINS
BLACKSHAW HEAD
③
④
CALDERDALE WAY
NEW DELIGHT PUB
⑤
SHAW BOTTOM
STAUPS MILL
Popples
Pry Hill
JUMBLE HOLE CLOUGH
Badger Lane
COLDEN WATER
②
UNDERBANK AVENUE
Den Farm
COLDEN CLOUGH
⑥
ROCHDALE CANAL
OLD MILL
Callis Wood
HELL HOLE ROCKS
Heptonstall
WC
A 646
⑦
SOCIAL AND BOWLING CLUB
STUBBING WHARF PUB
HOLME STREET
BUTTRESS
①
A 6033
Hebden Bridge

0   ½ mile
0   1 Km

Walk 46

Walk 46 Directions

① From the centre of **Hebden Bridge**, walk along **Holme Street** to the **Rochdale Canal**. Go right to follow the tow path beneath two bridges, past the **Stubbing Wharf** pub and beneath a railway bridge. Beyond the bridge the canal broadens; 200yds (183m) further on and before the next bridge, bear right and join a track right, to the A646.

② Cross the road and bear right for just 75yds (68m) to take **Underbank Avenue**, on the left, through an arch. Bear left again, past houses, to where another road comes through the viaduct. Go right on a track past a mill, and follow the beck up into the woodland of **Jumble Hole Clough**. Beyond a ruined mill, leave the track and bear left to cross the beck. Beyond a hairpin bend, climb steeply, passing a dam. When the track wheels left, keep ahead, now above the beck. Take a gate and cross the bottom of a field, to re-enter woodland. Keep ahead uphill, to a gap in a fence. Walk downhill, past the ruins of **Staups Mill**, then steeply up to cross a bridge. Take steps and cross a field to a waymark. Keep left, following a wall to a gate in front of **Hippins**.

③ Join the **Calderdale Way**, bearing right up a track between farm buildings to a stile. Follow a path to the next stile; then between a fence and a wall. Cross the track to **Apple Tree Farm**, to follow a line of causeway stones across three more stiles, passing to the right of a cottage. Cross the field to a gate at the right corner, then follow a causeway over a stile, and along a track to **Blackshaw Head**.

④ Go right, along the road, for 20yds (18m), to take a gate on the left. Bear half right across the field to a stile, then follow the right edge of the next field. Cross four more fields, and stiles, to a gate. Go left down a path, to **Shaw Bottom**. Keep left of the house to a metalled track.

⑤ Go right, along the track (or left for the **New Delight** pub). When the track bears left, keep ahead on a track. Look out for a marker post; go left here, down steps, and cross **Colden Water**. Climb up the other side, to follow a causeway right, at the top of woodland. At the second stile bear left to keep following the causeway. Keep right at a crossing of tracks, passing left of a house. Keep ahead, on a path downhill, at the next crossing of tracks, by a bench. Keep left at the next fork to a road.

⑥ Go left here, uphill; just before the road bears left, take a gap in the wall to the right. From here your path meanders through woodland. Emerge from the woodland, and follow a wall to **Hell Hole Rocks**.

⑦ Bear left at a wall-end, and cross an access road. At the junction turn right to the **Social and Bowling Club** (straight on for Walk 49). Go right, on a walled path and follow the wall to your left, downhill, soon through a spur of woodland and on to a track round to the left. Past houses you come to a road junction. Go left for 50yds (46m) and take the paved track right. This is the **Buttress**, taking you steeply down into **Hebden Bridge**.

> **WHERE TO EAT AND DRINK** ⓘ
> The **New Delight** is conveniently situated at the halfway point of the walk. Good beer, imaginative food and stone-flagged floors make it the ideal spot for lunch.

Walk 47

The Bridestone Rocks from Lydgate

Ancient tracks and gritstone outcrops, with terrific views of the steep-sided Cliviger Valley.

•DISTANCE•	5 miles (8km)
•MINIMUM TIME•	2hrs 30min
•ASCENT / GRADIENT•	984ft (300m) ▲▲▲
•LEVEL OF DIFFICULTY•	👫 👫 👫
•PATHS•	Moorland and packhorse paths, some quiet roads, 3 stiles
•LANDSCAPE•	Steep-sided valley and open moorland
•SUGGESTED MAP•	aqua3 OS Explorer OL21 South Pennines
•START / FINISH•	Grid reference: SD 924256
•DOG FRIENDLINESS•	Be careful around sheep grazing on the moorland
•PARKING•	Roadside parking in Lydgate, 1½ miles (2.4km) out of Todmorden, on A646, signposted to Burnley
•PUBLIC TOILETS•	None on route
•CONTRIBUTOR•	John Morrison

BACKGROUND TO THE WALK

The Long Causeway, between Halifax and Burnley, is an ancient trading route, possibly dating back to the Bronze Age. Crosses and waymarker stones helped to guide travellers across the moorland wastes, though most of them have been lost or damaged in the intervening years. Amazingly, Mount Cross has survived intact: a splendid, though crudely carved, example of the Celtic 'wheel-head' design. Opinions differ about its age but it is certainly the oldest man-made artefact in the area, erected at least a thousand years ago.

The Sportsman's Inn, visited on this walk, is one of many isolated pubs in the South Pennines that seem to be situated 'miles from anywhere'. In fact they were built on old routes, and catered for customers on the move, such as drovers and the men who led the trains of packhorse ponies across the moorland tracks. The Sportsman's Inn lies on the Long Causeway, now upgraded to a high-level road between Todmorden and Burnley. These days the pub caters for motorists and walkers, with good food and beers.

The Bridestones

The hills and moors to the north of Todmorden are dotted with gritstone outcrops. The impressive piles of Orchan Rocks and Whirlaw Rocks are both encountered on this walk. But the most intriguing rock formations are to be found at the Bridestones. One rock in particular has been weathered by wind and water into a tear-drop shape, and stands on a base that looks far too slender to support its great weight. It resembles a rock in the North York Moors National Park, which is also known as the Bridestone.

Cliviger Valley

The Cliviger Valley links two towns – Todmorden in West Yorkshire and Burnley in Lancashire – that expanded with the textile trade, and then suffered when that trade went into decline. The valley itself is narrow and steep-sided, in places almost a gorge. Into the cramped confines of the valley are shoe-horned the road, railway line, the infant River Calder and communities such as Portsmouth, Cornholme and Lydgate that grew up around the textile mills. The mills were powered by fast-flowing becks, running off the steep hillsides. The valley is almost a microcosm of the Industrial Revolution: by no means beautiful, but full of character. This area is particularly well provided with good footpaths, some of them still paved with their original causey stones.

Walk 47 Directions

① From the post office in **Lydgate**, take **Church Road**. At the end go right, down the drive towards a house. Look for a path that passes to the right of this house and soon goes beneath the railway arch. Join a track, as you walk uphill, the track is sunken, between walls. Where the

walls end, the track gives access to open moorland. Keep right, along a track towards a farm. Keep left of the farmhouse, continuing along a track uphill. When you meet another track, go right towards a rocky outcrop on the first horizon. Beyond two gates you are on open moor again: **Whirlaw Common**. Cross pasture on a causeway to a gate and **Whirlaw Stones**.

Walk 47

WHERE TO EAT AND DRINK ⓘ
The **Sportsman's Inn** is directly on the route of this walk. Better yet, it specialises in good food, as these isolated Pennine pubs now tend to do. The **Staff of Life**, on the main A646 at Lydgate, is another cosy 'real ale' pub where walkers get a warm welcome.

② Keep to the causeway that bears right, below the stones, with panoramic views of the **Cliviger Valley**, **Todmorden** and, ahead, **Stoodley Pike**. Leave **Whirlaw Common** by a gate on to a walled path. Bear sharp left at a farm, on a stony track that follows a wall uphill. Bear right around the rocks, to join **Windy Harbour Lane**. You have a steep climb, before the road levels off to meet **Eastwood Road**. Go left here for just 150yds (140m). Where the wall ends, take a stile on the left. A grassy path leads you to another fascinating collection of rocks, known as the **Bridestones**.

③ Continue past the **Bridestones** through a landscape of scattered boulders, before turning right to follow an indistinct path across rough terrain. When you meet a road, you'll be greeted by the sight of the **Sportsman's Inn**.

④ Go left, along the road; you have a mile (1.6km) of level walking, passing the **Hawks Stones** on the right and a handful of houses, until

WHILE YOU'RE THERE ⓘ
If you continue along the Long Causeway, you'll soon come to **Coal Clough Windfarm**. These huge wind turbines can be found on the crest of many a South Pennine hill, attracting strong winds and equally strong opinions. To some people they represent a sustainable future for energy, to others they are ugly intrusions in the landscape.

you come to a minor road on the left. This is **Mount Lane**, signed to **Shore** and **Todmorden**. Walk down this road and beyond a farm on the right, take a good track to the left, slightly downhill. Look out for **Mount Cross** in a field to your left.

⑤ Detour past **Lower Intake Farm** on a path, soon enclosed by walls. 200yds (183m) beyond a small bridge over a stream, look out for a stile on your right, by a gate between heavy stone gateposts. Follow a field path downhill, keeping a wall to your left. This grassy track takes you beneath another gritstone outcrop, known as **Orchan Rocks**.

WHAT TO LOOK FOR ⓘ
In geological terms, the South Pennines are largely made up of millstone grit and coarse sandstone. Where the gritstone is visible, it forms rocky crags and outcrops, like those encountered on this walk. The typical landscape is moorland of heather and peat, riven by steep-sided valleys. Here, in the cramped confines of the steep-sided Cliviger Valley, road, rail and river cross and re-cross each other – like the flex of an old-fashioned telephone.

⑥ Where the wall bears left, beyond the rocks, follow it downhill to a stile. You now join a farm track that takes a serpentine route downhill, through woodland. Your way is clear: down into the valley and back into **Lydgate**.

Along Langfield Edge to Stoodley Pike

A classic South Pennine ridge walk to a much-loved landmark.

•DISTANCE•	7 miles (11.3km)
•MINIMUM TIME•	3hrs 30min
•ASCENT / GRADIENT•	1,017ft (310m) ▲▲▲
•LEVEL OF DIFFICULTY•	🚶 🚶 🚶
•PATHS•	Good paths and tracks, 3 stiles
•LANDSCAPE•	Open moorland
•SUGGESTED MAP•	aqua3 OS Explorer OL21 South Pennines
•START / FINISH•	Grid reference: SD 936242
•DOG FRIENDLINESS•	Under control as sheep present throughout
•PARKING•	Free parking in centre of Todmorden
•PUBLIC TOILETS•	By bus station in Todmorden
•CONTRIBUTOR•	John Morrison

BACKGROUND TO THE WALK

Todmorden – call it 'Tod' if you want to sound like a local – is a border town, standing at the junction of three valley routes. Before the town was included in the old West Riding, the Yorkshire/Lancashire border divided the town in two. Todmorden's splendid town hall, built in an unrestrained classical Greek style, reflects this dual personality. On top of the town hall are carved figures which represent, on one side, the Lancashire cotton trade, and, on the other side, Yorkshire agriculture and engineering.

Stoodley Pike

Stoodley Pike is a ubiquitous sight around the Calder Valley, an unmistakable landmark. It seems you only need to turn a corner, or crest a hill, and it appears on the horizon. West Yorkshire is full of monuments built on prominent outcrops, but few of them dominate the view in quite the way that Stoodley Pike does.

In 1814, a trio of patriotic Todmorden men convened in a local pub, the Golden Lion. Now that the Napoleonic War was over, they wanted to commemorate the peace with a suitably grand monument. So they organised a public subscription, and raised enough money to erect a monument, 1,476ft (450m) up on Langfield Edge, overlooking the town. Construction was halted, briefly, when Napoleon rallied his troops, and was not completed until the following year, when he was finally defeated at the Battle of Waterloo. This original monument was undone by the Pennine weather. Ironically, it collapsed in 1854, on the very day that the Crimean War broke out. Another group of local worthies came together (yes, at the Golden Lion again) to raise more money. So the Stoodley Pike we see today is Mark II: 131ft (40m) high and built to commemorate the ending of hostilities in the Crimea.

Stoodley Pike remains visible for almost every step of this exhilarating ridge walk. As well as being a favourite destination for local walkers, the Pike is visited by the Pennine Way. Remember to pack a torch for this walk. By climbing a flight of unlit steps inside the monument, you emerge at a viewing platform offering panoramic views over Calderdale.

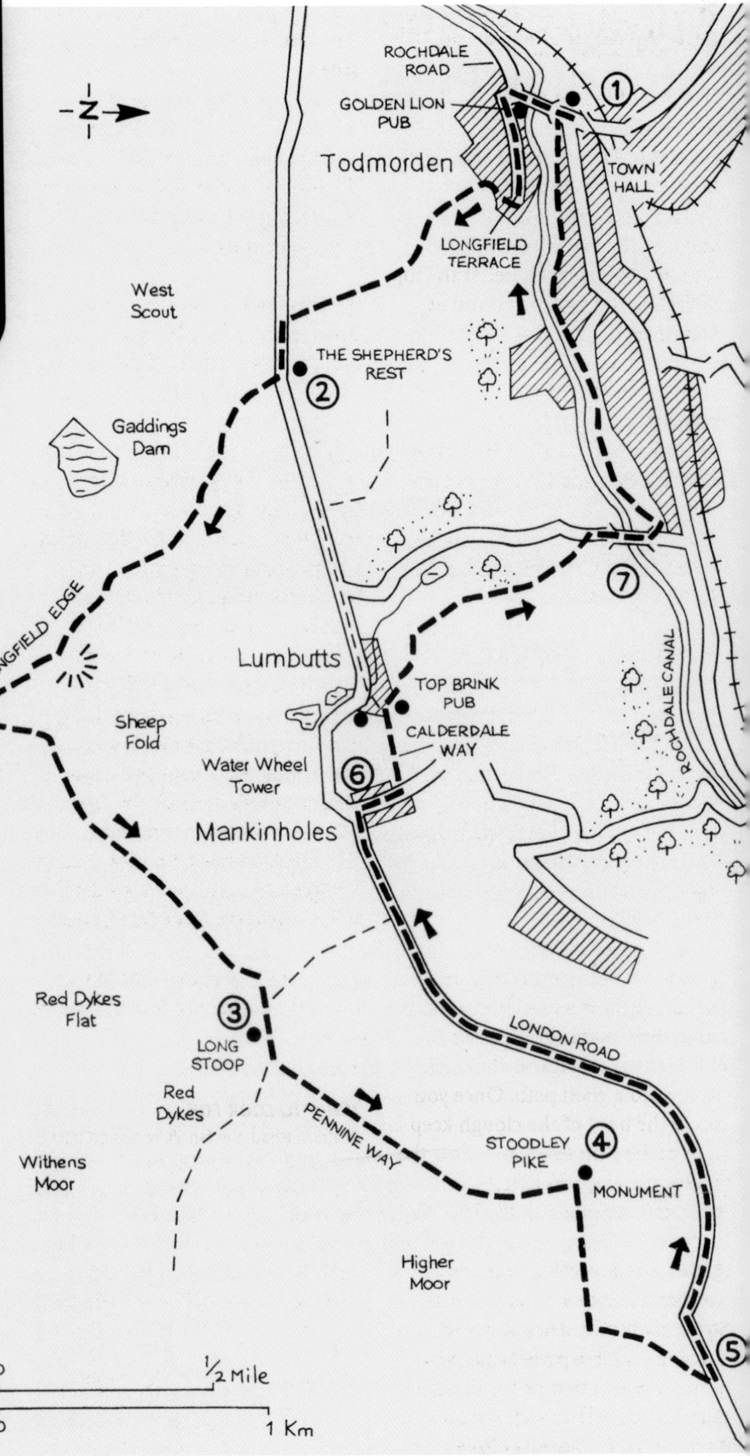

ROCHDALE ROAD

GOLDEN LION PUB

① TOWN HALL

Todmorden

LONGFIELD TERRACE

West Scout

THE SHEPHERD'S REST ②

Gaddings Dam

⑦

LANGFIELD EDGE

Lumbutts

TOP BRINK PUB

CALDERDALE WAY

Sheep Fold

Water Wheel Tower

Mankinholes ⑥

ROCHDALE CANAL

Red Dykes Flat

③ LONG STOOP

Red Dykes

LONDON ROAD

Withens Moor

PENNINE WAY

STOODLEY PIKE ④ MONUMENT

Higher Moor

⑤

N

0 ½ Mile

0 1 Km

Walk 48 Directions

① From the town hall in the centre of **Todmorden**, take the **Rochdale road** (A6033), cross the canal, and bear left immediately after the **Golden Lion** pub. Walk up the road and take the first road on the left, to avoid a housing estate. At the top of the hill the road peters out at **Longfield Terrace**. Take a track to the left, to find yourself suddenly 'on the tops'. When the track forks, keep left to a farm building, from where you will get the first glimpse of your destination – **Stoodley Pike** – on the horizon ahead. Continue along the farm track to a road. Go left, to find a pub, the **Shepherd's Rest,** in splendid isolation.

WHERE TO EAT AND DRINK ⓘ

Despite the rugged nature of this walk you have a choice of pubs. The isolated **Shepherd's Rest** is near the beginning, while the **Top Brink** in Lumbutts is towards the end. If you want to sit in the pub where the raising of Stoodley Pike was first discussed, you must wait until you have finished the walk: the **Golden Lion** is in Todmorden, close to the canal.

---

② Opposite the pub, take a track leading through a gate, uphill, on to **Langfield Common**. Keep left at old quarry workings, as the track narrows to a good path. Once you round the head of the clough keep right as the path forks, to follow the ridge top, **Langfield Edge,** with views of **Calderdale** to the left.

③ There is a meeting of paths by a waymarker stone known as **Long Stoop**. Continue straight ahead, crossing a superb paved causeway, on what is a section of the **Pennine Way**. You have level walking now until you reach **Stoodley Pike**.

④ Walk past the monument, as the path bears right, downhill, to a gap stile in a wall. After just 50yds (46m), take a ladder stile in an adjacent wall to the left. Continue downhill to meet a track. You leave the route of the **Pennine Way** here, by walking left along the wide and well-made track.

⑤ This track, known as **London Road**, offers a long but gentle descent to a road. Go right, into the hamlet of **Mankinholes**.

⑥ About 100yds (91m) beyond the last house, take a paved, walled track on the left, signed 'Calderdale Way', that emerges at the **Top Brink** pub in another tiny settlement, **Lumbutts**. Bear right to take a path between houses and follow a section of causeway on a path between a fence and a wall. At a gap stile in a wall, head right, slightly uphill, across a field to another gap stile. Your path now leads downhill through the steep-sided valley. Join a farm track, downhill, and meet a minor road by cottages. Go right, passing a derelict mill, to cross the **Rochdale Canal**.

⑦ Join the tow path to the left, to follow the canal back into the centre of **Todmorden**.

WHAT TO LOOK FOR ⓘ

London Road, the fancifully named track you follow from Stoodley Pike down into Mankinholes, was a 'cotton famine road'. When the cotton trade suffered one of its periodic slumps, mill owner John Fielden of Todmorden put some of his men to work on building this road, so he could ride his carriage up to Stoodley Pike. Fielden also built Dobroyd Castle, its castellated turrets looking slightly out of place on a hill overlooking the town. This is now a Buddhist retreat.

Hardcastle Crags and Crimsworth Dean

A pair of beautiful wooded valleys, linked by a high level path.

•DISTANCE•	5 miles (8km)
•MINIMUM TIME•	2hrs 30min
•ASCENT / GRADIENT•	787ft (240m) ▲▲ ▲▲
•LEVEL OF DIFFICULTY•	🚶🚶 🚶🚶 🚶
•PATHS•	Good paths and tracks, plus open pasture, no stiles
•LANDSCAPE•	Woodland, fields and moorland fringe
•SUGGESTED MAP•	aqua3 OS Explorer OL21 South Pennines
•START / FINISH•	Grid reference: SD 988291
•DOG FRIENDLINESS•	Plenty of opportunities for dogs to be off lead
•PARKING•	National Trust pay-and-display car parks at Midgehole, near Hebden Bridge (accessible via A6033, Keighley Road)
•PUBLIC TOILETS•	Near car park
•CONTRIBUTOR•	John Morrison

BACKGROUND TO THE WALK

Hebden Bridge, just 4 miles (6.4km) from the Yorkshire/Lancashire border, has been a popular place to visit ever since the railway was extended across the Pennines, through the Calder Valley. But those train passengers weren't coming for a day out in a grimy little mill town; the big attraction was the wooded valley of Hebden Dale – usually called 'Hardcastle Crags' – just a short charabanc ride away. 'Hebden Bridge for Hardcastle Crags' was the stationmaster's cry, as trains approached the station. Here were shady woods, easy riverside walks and places to spread out a picnic blanket. To people who lived in the terraced streets of Bradford, Leeds or Halifax, Hardcastle Crags must have seemed idyllic. The steep-sided valley reminded Swiss visitors of their own country, and became 'Little Switzerland' – at least to the writers of tourist brochures. The only disappointment, in fact, was the crags themselves: unassuming gritstone outcrops, almost hidden by trees.

Industrial Demands

The Industrial Revolution created a huge demand for water: for mills, factories and domestic use. To quench the thirst of the rapidly expanding textile towns, many steep-sided valleys, known in the South Pennines as cloughs, were dammed to create reservoirs. Six of these lie within easy walking distance of Hardcastle Crags. They represented huge feats of civil engineering by the hundreds of navvies who built them, around the end of the 19th century, with picks and shovels. The men were housed in a shanty town, known as Dawson City and both men and materials were transported to the work-sites by a convoluted steam-powered railway system that crossed the valley on an elaborate wooden viaduct.

Hardcastle Crags escaped the indignity of being turned into a reservoir, but it was touch and go. Three times during the last 50 years (the last time was in 1970) plans were drawn up to flood the valley. And three times, thankfully, wiser counsels prevailed and the plans were turned down. Lord Savile, a major landowner in the area, once owned the valley.

It was he who supplemented the natural woodland with plantings of new trees – particularly pines, and laid out the walks and the carriage drive. In 1948 Lord Savile donated Hardcastle Crags, and the nearby valley of Crimsworth Dean, to the National Trust. Because of this bequeathment, the future of this delightful valley looks secure and local people will continue to enjoy this valuable amenity.

Hardcastle Crags are a haven for wildlife. Bird watchers can look out for pied flycatchers, woodpeckers, jays, sparrowhawks and the ubiquitous dipper. In spring there are displays of bluebells; in summer the woods are filled with bird-song; the beech woods are a riot of colour as the leaves turn each autumn.

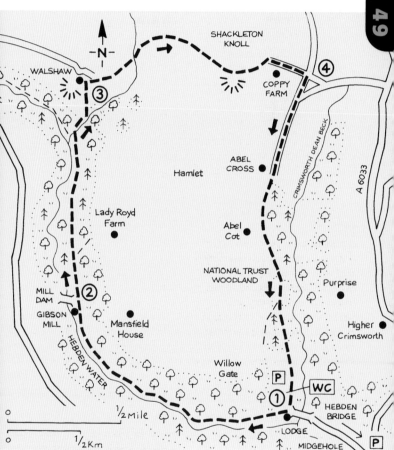

Walk 49 Directions

① Walk up the drive, passing the lodge, and into the woods. Take the first path to the left, which descends to **Hebden Water**. Follow a good riverside path through delectable woodland, passing **Hebden Hey** –

a popular picnic site, with stepping stones – to reach **Gibson Mill**. The buildings, and mill dam behind, are worth investigating.

② For this longer walk you join the track uphill, to the right of **Gibson Mill**, soon passing the crags that give the woods their name.

Walk 49

WHILE YOU'RE THERE ⓘ

Walk the old road from Hebden Bridge to Haworth (it's marked as such on the OS map) that includes the section of track through wooded Crimsworth Dean. The old road is never hard to find, and offers easy walking with terrific views all the way. Have lunch in Haworth, and take the easy way back to Hebden Bridge – by bus.

Keep on the main track, ignoring side-paths, to leave woodland and meet a metalled road. Keep left here, still uphill, across a beck and approach **Walshaw**, a knot of houses enjoying terrific views.

③ Just before you reach the houses – when you are opposite some barns – bear sharp right through a gate on to an enclosed track (signed to **Crimsworth Dean**). You are soon on a grassy track across pasture, descending to a beck and through a gate. Walk uphill, soon bearing to the right as you follow a wall around the shoulder of **Shackleton Knoll**. Go through a gate in the wall on your left, and continue as the path bears right, still following the wall, but now it's on your right. Here you have level walking and great views. Take a gate in a wall on the right, just above **Coppy Farm**, to join a walled track downhill into the valley of

Crimsworth Dean. You meet a more substantial track by another ruin of a farm. This track is the old road from **Hebden Bridge** to **Haworth**: a great walk to contemplate for another day.

④ Bear right, along this elevated track, passing a farm on the left. Look out, by a farm access track to the right, for **Abel Cross**: not one but a pair of old waymarker stones. Continue down the main track, into National Trust woodland, keeping left, after a field, when the track forks. Beyond a pair of cottages the track is metalled; you soon arrive back at the car parks at **Midgehole**.

WHAT TO LOOK FOR ⓘ

Hebden Water rushes attractively through the wooded valley of Hardcastle Crags. These upland rivers and streams are the perfect habitat for an attractive little bird called the **dipper**. Dark brown, with a blaze of white on the breast, the dipper never strays from water. Unique among British birds, it has perfected the trick of walking underwater.

WHERE TO EAT AND DRINK ⓘ

The **Packhorse Inn** can be found on the unclassified road between Colden and Brierfield, just beyond the wooded valley of Hardcastle Crags. The Packhorse is one of many solitary, exposed pubs to be found in Pennine Yorkshire, which existed to cater for the drovers and packhorse men. There's a warm welcome for walkers, and hearty meals. In winter, though, the pub only opens at lunchtimes at the weekend.

Halifax and the Shibden Valley

See an old packhorse track, a superb half-timbered hall and a hidden valley.

•DISTANCE•	4½ miles (7.2km)
•MINIMUM TIME•	2hrs 30min
•ASCENT / GRADIENT•	410ft (125m) ▲▲▲
•LEVEL OF DIFFICULTY•	秫 秫 秫
•PATHS•	Old packhorse tracks and field paths, no stiles
•LANDSCAPE•	Surprisingly rural, considering the proximity to Halifax
•SUGGESTED MAP•	aqua3 OS Explorer 288 Bradford & Huddersfield
•START / FINISH•	Grid reference: SE 095254
•DOG FRIENDLINESS•	Keep on lead crossing busy roads
•PARKING•	In Halifax
•PUBLIC TOILETS•	Halifax (near bus station)
•CONTRIBUTOR•	John Morrison

BACKGROUND TO THE WALK

Set amongst the Pennine hills, Halifax was a town in the vanguard of the Industrial Revolution. Its splendid civic buildings and huge mills are a good indication of the town's prosperity, won from the woollen trade. Ironically, the most splendid building of all came close to being demolished. The Piece Hall, built in 1779, predates the industrial era. Here, in a total of 315 rooms on three colonnaded floors, the hand-weavers of the district would offer their wares (known as 'pieces') for sale to cloth merchants. The collonades surround a massive square. Your first reaction on walking into the square may be surprise, for this is a building that would not look out of place in Renaissance Italy.

The mechanisation of the weaving process left the Piece Hall largely redundant. In the intervening years it has served a variety of purposes, including as a venue for political oration and as a wholesale market. During the 1970s, having narrowly escaped the wrecking ball, the Piece Hall was spruced up and given a new lease of life. Now it houses a museum, tourist information centre and a number of small shops and businesses. But the buildings full potential as a tourist attraction has yet to be realised.

The Magna Via

The cobbled thoroughfare that climbs so steeply up Beacon Hill is known as the Magna Via. Until 1741, when a turnpike road was built, this was the only practicable approach to Halifax from the east, for both foot and packhorse traffic. Also known as Wakefield Gate, the Magna Via linked up with the Long Causeway, the old high level road to Burnley. That intrepid 18th-century traveller, Daniel Defoe, was one of those who struggled up this hill. 'We quitted Halifax not without some astonishment at its situation, being so surrounded with hills, and those so high as makes the coming in and going out of it exceedingly troublesome'. The route was superseded in the 1820s by the turnpike constructed through Godley Cutting. Today the Magna Via, too steep to be adopted for modern motor vehicles, remains a fascinating relic of the past.

Shibden Hall

Situated on a hill above Halifax, this magnificent half-timbered house is set in 90 acres (36ha) of beautiful, rolling parkland. Dating from 1420, the hall has been owned by prominent local families – the Oates, Saviles, Waterhouses and, latterly, the Listers. All these families left their mark on the fabric of the house, but, the core of the original house remains intact. The rooms are furnished in period style, to show how they might have looked over almost six centuries. The oak furniture and panelling has that patina of age that antique forgers try in vain to emulate. Barns and other outbuildings have been converted into a folk museum, with displays of old vehicles, tools and farm machinery.

When Emily Brontë created Thrushcross Grange in her only novel *Wuthering Heights*, she may have had Shibden Hall in mind. It certainly proved a suitable location in 1991 for a new film version of the famous story, which starred Ralph Fiennes as Heathcliffe and Juliette Binoche as Cathy.

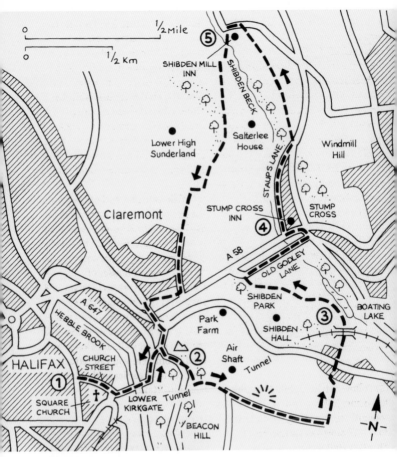

Walk 50 Directions

① Walk downhill, past a tall spire that once belonged to **Square Church**, and down **Church Street**, passing the smoke-blackened parish church. Bear left on to **Lower Kirkgate**, then right on to **Bank Bottom**. Cross **Hebble Brook** and walk uphill; where the road bears sharp left, keep straight ahead up a steep cobbled lane. When you meet a road, go right for about 200yds (183m). Just after the entrance to a warehouse (Aquaspersion), take a cobbled path on the left that makes a steep ascent up **Beacon Hill**.

② This old packhorse track – known as the **Magna Via** – joins another path and continues uphill to a large retaining wall, where you have a choice of tracks. Keep left on a cinder track, slightly downhill, as views open up of the surprisingly rural **Shibden Valley**. Keep left when the track forks again; after a further 100yds (91m) take a walled path on the left (signed to **Stump Cross**). Follow a hedgerow downhill through a little estate of new houses to a road. Cross here and take a gated path immediately to the right of a farm entrance, which takes you downhill, under the railway line and into **Shibden Park**, close to the boating lake.

> **WHILE YOU'RE THERE** ⓘ
>
> As well as the **Piece Hall**, which houses an art gallery and several craft shops, you should acquire a child and visit **Eureka!**, the ultimate in hands-on discovery museums. It is designed specifically for children up to the age of 12, with over 400 interactive exhibits exploring science, nature and the world around you.

③ Follow a drive uphill. Near the top of the hill you will find a footpath on the left, giving access to the Elizabethan splendour of **Shibden Hall** itself. Otherwise, continue uphill; just before you meet the main A58 road, bear right, down **Old Godley Lane**. Pass houses and take steps up to the main road at the busy junction of **Stump Cross**.

> **WHERE TO EAT AND DRINK** ⓘ
>
> At the half-way point of this walk you have the good fortune to start the return leg from **Shibden Mill Inn**. Tucked away in a leafy corner of Shibden Dale, yet close to the centre of Halifax, this picturesque inn enjoys the best of both worlds. A sympathetic reworking of an old mill, this is the place for good food and, when the weather is kind, a drink in the beer garden.

④ Cross over the road and take **Staups Lane**, to the left of the **Stump Cross Inn**. Walk up the lane, which soon becomes cobbled, to meet another surfaced road. Bear left here, down a metalled track, through a gate, to join a straight, double-paved track into **Shibden Dale**. When the paving ends, continue via a gate and through open pasture. Turn left, at the next gate, walking down a lane that soon leads you to the **Shibden Mill Inn**.

⑤ Walk to the far end of the pub's car park, to join a track that crosses **Shibden Beck**. Beyond a brick-built house, the track narrows to a walled path. You emerge from countryside, to walk past the houses of **Claremont** and cross the main A58 road, as it goes through the steep-sided **Godley Cutting**, on a bridge. Take a set of steps immediately after the bridge and walk left along the road. From here you can retrace your route of earlier in the day, back into **Halifax**.

> **WHAT TO LOOK FOR** ⓘ
>
> The birds-eye view of Halifax from **Beacon Hill** is well worth the effort of climbing it. A century ago this view would have looked very different: most people's idea of William Blake's 'dark satanic mills' were here in unhealthy profusion, casting a dense pall of sulphurous smoke over the valley.

50 Walks in

The following titles are also available in this series

Acknowledgements

AQUA3 AA Publishing and Outcrop Publishing Services would like to thank Chartech for supplying aqua3 maps for this book.
For more information visit their website: www.aqua3.com.

Series management: Outcrop Publishing Services Limited, Cumbria
Series editor: Chris Bagshaw
Copy editor: Pam Stagg
Front cover: AA Photo Library/D Tarn